A STROKE OF LUCK

My Journey Through A Traumatic Brain Injury

Aithal

Version 1.0

Copyright © 2025 Aithal

All rights reserved.

For beloved parents,
Suhas and Anant

To the love of my life, my wife, Minoo
You complete me.

Preface

On October 23, 2000, I had a massive stroke. When rushed to the hospital, I was given a fifty percent chance of survival. I was thirty-six, my wife thirty-four, my daughter ten, and my son just over one.

I'm not a writer. I merely want to narrate my experience, my story of the ups and downs of life, and how it's vital to have a supportive family and good friends. After all, they are my only support in this country. The rest of my family is in India. My wife and I, along with our two children, are the only nuclear family in the US.

This is not fiction. Everything described in this book has happened to me over the years after my stroke.

There are two avatars of me: one before my stroke and one after. They both have different personalities and outlook towards life.

I believe the way one looks at life is important. I could feel sorry for myself and give up, or I could consider myself fortunate to be surrounded by loved ones. I chose the latter.

I have always thought about how lucky I am (hence the title of this book). I have a 'never-give-up' attitude towards life. In fact, I wrote an article many years ago in a magazine for those who've had TBI (Traumatic Brain Injury) to inspire them. Looking back, that it was a little premature as I'd not experienced the many things I can now share with you.

There are several lessons I've learned over the years. But the foremost one is to appreciate life. It's very fragile, and mine turned —turning my world upside down—in fifteen seconds.

Therefore, my dear reader, do not take yours for granted. Enjoy every moment it has given you. In the age of social media and the ubiquity of mobile devices, we tend to forget the human connection. Our heads are buried in a small screen to seek gratification and validation from strangers while the people we know are right before us. Albeit, they, too, are doing the same. But I digress. Let me climb down from my preachy podium to narrate my experience.

The biggest mistake many who have had a TBI make—at least, I made—is to compare yourself now with yourself before the stroke. Only when you make a mental shift to think of how long you have come from that disastrous day, will you start feeling charged about what lies ahead and how you can make the most of it to make yourself better.

You could look at it as a glass half-empty or half-full. It's in your attitude. As you can guess, I'm the glass-half-full kind. Also, I must say that this country's infrastructure and facilities are far superior than I would have experienced had I been elsewhere. On that fateful day, when I had my stroke, fortunately, I was at home. My wife dialed 911, and, within three minutes (one hundred eighty seconds), there was a police car, a fire engine, and an ambulance in front of my house. If I had not received immediate care, I doubt that I would have survived. Ergo, you wouldn't be reading this book.

I'd always wanted to ride in one of those emergency vehicles with the sirens blaring. Little did I foresee that I would do that, fighting for my life. Come to think of it, at the time, I wasn't aware of the siren.

Along the journey of the past 24 years, many have touched my life. They may not be aware, but I am, of how they have made an impact on me.

I have been extremely blessed and fortunate to see my children grow up and attend their graduations. I have also been lucky to participate in several weddings, graduation parties, etc. But above all, I've been fortunate to have visited India several times and seen several other countries. This was only possible because of my wife.

I sincerely hope that this book inspires folks with a TBI. Although each TBI is different and affects different brain regions, and the severity varies, I'm sure that most individuals who have the misfortune of a TBI go through a similar (although varying) experience. Over the years, I've seen folks with different degrees of severity of a stroke in many support groups. Many of them have no apparent physical symptoms, but their mental ability has been affected. My stroke, on the other hand, impacted me physically. Fortunately, my cognitive faculties are still intact (however, some may disagree).

The other silver lining is that I've given up smoking. I asked my doctors if that could be the cause. They said 'no,' but it's still debated. My wife, who has always disliked my habit, maintains that smoking exacerbated my stroke, and I'm afraid I have to disagree. However, it's a moot point. The result is that I've not felt a cigarette on my lips for the past twenty-four years. I have more energy, breathe better, taste better, smell better, etc.

There are so many other advantages (not counting the dent in my pocket.). In fact, my nose is now more sensitive to the foul odor of a cigarette. I was forced to go cold turkey due to my prolonged stay at the hospital. I was too ill to notice any physical withdrawal symptoms. However, I can attest that it was a mental challenge. Otherwise, I don't know if I could have easily kicked the habit.

When I was all by myself, as the adage goes, an idle mind is the devil's workshop; the 'devil' side of my brain would coax, cajole, barter to cut a deal, etc. *There's nothing wrong with one drag. When you go out, you'll see many patients smoking, and they all are fine. A tiny little drag is perfectly acceptable.* STOP IT, the 'saint' side would intervene. So, yes, in my opinion, it's a nasty and expensive habit. And I'm glad that I have given it up. Besides, it's much easier to refrain from smoking as most of the structures, planes, restaurants, etc., prohibit smoking.

> As a side note, having traveled to India several times, I've noticed that the government's approach to tackling this issue is much more direct and aggressive. Instead of using ambiguous words on the cigarette labels—often dictated by the tobacco industry, they use more impactful language. But again, I digress.

My message is: NEVER GIVE UP. NEVER. You will go through the ups and downs of life, the inner turmoils, a rollercoaster of emotions ranging from frustration to anger to despair. The journey could be long and arduous, but my dear reader (if you are one of the unfortunate victims of a TBI), believe me, there's a light at the end of the tunnel. After all, as a wise man once said, *excuses* make today easy, but tomorrow hard. And *discipline* makes today hard, but it makes tomorrow easy.

I recently turned sixty and, reflecting, I realized how far I have come. It has been a challenging journey but gratifying. Come along with me as I take a stroll down my memory lane. I'd consider it a success if I can make a difference in just one life.

Like an earthquake—and yes, being in California, I've gone through many—one never knows where and when a stroke can strike. There is no warning. Thus, there are no precautions I could take. Besides, I was too young to have one.

The most frustrating aspect is that my body refused to obey my brain. I had to retrain it. That required a tremendous amount of patience and repetitive actions. I had to get out of my comfort zone to feel confident again.

I hope my experience helps those who have had the same experience. I want them to know that they are not alone. Many have gone through it. It's not easy. However, their attitude and how they deal with the situation mentally can put them on a path to recovery. After all, God helps those who help themselves. There's nowhere to go from here but up. Sure, there will be a period of hopelessness. Sure, it's a long journey. Along the way, you'll meet many challenges, but how you tackle them will make a day or night difference. A thing that may be trivial to a regular person can be an uphill task for you. Please take it as a personal challenge and see how it feels when you accomplish it. Like you, I, too, had many hurdles to overcome. Know that there's a light at the end of the tunnel.

You are no longer in a hundred-meter sprint; you are now in a marathon. So, pace yourself and know you'll always get a second wind. And just like in a marathon, where there are many spectators along the way offering the runner a cup of water, you too will meet many of them willing to offer you help. Please take it. The harder you work, the luckier you'll get.

Come join me down my memory lane. Who knows … you may pick up a thing or two from my experience.

Chapter 1

October 23, 2000

IT WAS AROUND 11 A.M. on Monday. I was hurriedly working on my computer in my home office in Southern California, connected to my client's midrange computer in Central Oregon. I was busy finishing the program I was debugging and was due to fly to Oregon on Wednesday for a final presentation to a school district.

I had already spent two weeks feverishly putting the finishing touches to the presentation with my client, Vern. Having done this in my first job in the U.S., I was familiar with the process: prepare the flashcards for the routine—check; connect my terminal to the projector—check; *go through the sequence of screens I would be presenting—check.*

When I was at my client's site, I was working hard, burning the midnight oil to finish a project for a local school district. I would get up early in the morning, and my client would pick me up from the motel where I was staying and work till late evening. I had tirelessly done this for two weeks (including weekends) from pre-dawn to way past dusk. The only time I took in the beauty of Central Oregon was when I took a smoke break or went out for lunch with Vern. Our office was in a valley, surrounded by green meadows and snow-capped mountains beyond, with railway tracks going through the center of the flat valley. It was a stark difference from the hustle-bustle of city life in L.A. I would always enjoy going there and look forward to the change. The change of environment, fresh air, and the simplicity of a country lifestyle invigorated me. Also, having always been in a city—Mumbai to New York to Fort Lauderdale to Los Angeles, going there was like a whole new world had opened up. Hunting, fishing, boating, etc., were alien concepts to me—something I would witness on TV. The slow rhythm of country life was very different than the fast-paced life I was used to. Going there was like a working vacation for me.

However, I needed a break. I needed some downtime to recharge my batteries, enjoy home-cooked meals, enjoy family life, play with my son, etc.

Just when everything seemed to be in order, Vern asked me to modify the presentation slightly.

"That will involve me changing the program," I told him.

"How long will it take?" he asked.

"About a day."

I wanted to stay back in Oregon and keep working. However, my wife, being a Gujarati, vetoed it. It was a very auspicious day for her.

"It's *Dhanteras on Tuesday*," she told me over the phone. "I don't want you to spend the night alone in a motel. Fly in on Sunday and fly back on Wednesday."

"But it doesn't make sense to fly back just for three days."

"Nothing doing. You are coming back. And besides, we all miss you. Don't you want to see us?" She had guilted me, so reluctantly, I agreed. Besides, she was right. I missed them.

I told Vern, "I'm flying home tomorrow but'll return on Wednesday. I'll log into the system remotely and finish the program."

Reluctantly, he agreed. So, I'd flown back to Orange County, California, on Sunday. Now, Monday, I was glad to be back.

Looking back on that fateful day, I always shudder when I think about what could have happened to me had I been alone in a motel room in Oregon.

The country life is beautiful, but the city can offer more resources. I remember the office in Oregon was located in a small town. For us to have lunch, we would drive for a few miles to the next town. The scenery is breathtaking, but the facilities are sparse.

My wife was in the kitchen while I was typing away at my keyboard in my home office; my ten-year-old daughter was at school, and my fourteen-month-old son was playing in our family room. I decided that I needed a break. My body craved a nicotine fix. (Little did I know then that it was my last cigarette.) I had tried to kick the nasty habit several times in the past. However, each time—and I'm not proud to admit it, I failed. I went to the restroom and lit a cigarette. After inhaling a few puffs and blowing the smoke, I chucked the half-smoked butt in the toilet bowl, where it extinguished the moment it hit the water. I stood before the washbasin and looked at my reflection in the mirror. I raked my hand through my hair.

Something wasn't right.

Suddenly, I felt a warm sensation at the nape of my neck. Ignoring it, I turned on the faucet, collected cold water in the crook of my palm, and splashed it at the back of my neck, where the warm feeling was. I had done this before, and it had worked. However, this time, it didn't work. The throbbing wouldn't subside; in fact, it was rapidly increasing, coupled with a buzzing noise in my head. Now, I was feeling faint. The entire restroom was spinning. I held onto the edge of the washbasin to steady myself. Gingerly, I walked to our living room and collapsed with a thud on our rust-colored leather sofa. *Calm down*, I said to myself. *Maybe I shouldn't have smoked. Just sit here for a while to regain your composure. The feeling will subside.* However, it didn't.

On the contrary, the warmth that was concentrated at the base of my neck was spreading across my face. My stomach was growling. I felt like throwing up. But the last time I had a meal was last night. There would be nothing to throw up but coffee. My head was still throbbing. I could feel my heart beating faster against my chest. I thought I would pass out in a few seconds.

I screamed for my wife. "*Minoo*."

"What?" she yelled back from the kitchen.

"Come here."

She came to the living room and raised her eyebrows quizzically. "What is it?"

"Something's happening to me. I feel light-headed."

She gazed at me casually. Her expression didn't appear to be concerning. To her, there was an explanation. "Oh, it's nothing," she said. "It's because you've not had anything since you woke up. All you've had is coffee. Just rest for a little while."

She turned around to go back to the kitchen.

"No." By then, the warmth was spreading through my head. I was struggling to speak. My tongue felt thick in my mouth. I could hear my words slurring. "It's more than that. I shink I'm having a shtroke."

"*What?*" She stopped, turned around, and looked at me incredulously. She knows me very well. I'm not a complainer. I have a high tolerance level for pain. I don't bother to tell her of minor aches and pains. I'd rather tough it out. But she realized that it was different this time. I could see her look of surprise mixed with fear.

"Y-yesh," I wailed. It was becoming increasingly difficult to speak. The throbbing was increasing even more, feeling like it was wedged in-between two iron plates and someone was tightening the screws. Within seconds, my upper torso dropped from sitting on one side of the sofa. I started to throw up, and my right side froze. I was unable to speak any further. All I could do to convey my pain was to scream.

My wife's face contorted in fear. She sprang into action. She ran to the kitchen and dialed 911. "My husband is having a stroke," she screamed a moment later, her voice trembling with fear.

I remember the front door opening in minutes. (I was later informed that the police, the ambulance, and the fire engine were at my doorsteps within three minutes.) Looking back, I realize that timely attendance saved my life. I've heard of so many horror stories where people have lost their lives due to the lack of such robust infrastructure.

Although events were racing, I felt everything was happening slowly. I have sporadic memories of the happenings since then, to my being wheeled into the emergency room. Two firemen lifted me (or were they paramedics? I don't remember, as they both wore blue). I was gently placed on a stretcher. The stretcher was placed on a gurney that slid into the ambulance.

My wife clambered in the back with me. Fortunately, we had a maid coming to help us at that time. She took care of my son while my wife accompanied me. Although I was conscious, my head was still pounding. There was a constant buzzing sound. The pain was unbearable.

I could hear the medics talking on their communication equipment with the hospital to which I was being taken. However, they were informed that it wasn't equipped to handle such emergency cases, so I was to be taken to Long Beach Memorial instead.

I didn't have a choice. I would have to endure the pain a little longer.

Long Beach Memorial

After what seemed to be an eternity, the ambulance halted. The back doors swung open, and I was slid out into a gurney. The sun was beating down on my already hot face and wasn't helping me. I squinted to attempt to shield my eyes. In a few seconds, to my relief, I was wheeled to the cool emergency room. I blinked my eyes to adjust them to the interior. However, since I was lying flat on the gurney, there wasn't much I could take in. All I could do was to rely on my ears. That, too, didn't sound very clear. Distant-sounding muffled voices, beeps of monitors, the typical smell of disinfectants and antiseptics, shiny sky-blue walls and polished white floors reflecting the bright white lights, etc., told me I was in a hospital. A sterile place that one associates with it.

I remember it being surprisingly quiet—almost eerie—precisely the opposite of the noisy atmosphere, people shouting, patients moaning out of pain as they were shifted from a gurney to a bed, doctors barking orders to the nursing staff, a monitor rapidly beeping to indicate that someone's pulse or heart rate was increasing, etc., that I've seen on a TV show. There was no chaos, no running around, attending to one patient after another. I'm not saying it didn't happen, but it didn't happen where I was taken.

The emergency room doctors didn't know the extent of the damage. The foremost thing to attend to was to stabilize me. It was evident from my contorted face that I had a severe brain injury. Yes, I had a stroke and a Traumatic Brain Injury (TBI), but the brain is a vast and complex network of rapidly firing neurons. It was vital to know which part of my brain was affected. This could only happen after an MRI scan, but that could only happen after I was stabilized.

Besides, it was vital to determine if it was an aneurysm—the one I had or a blood clot. The latter is much easier to reverse by administering blood thinners. However, giving the same treatment to someone with an aneurysm that has ruptured can be fatal. Thus, they could not provide me with any medication to treat my symptoms until an MRI was performed on my brain.

To make matters worse, I was screaming in pain. I don't know, but I assume a team of doctors and nurses were rushing to my aid. Usually, it is easier to diagnose a symptom when a wound is external. However, I had no visible injuries, no blood gushing from a wound, etc. There is nothing to help them make a correct diagnosis. The only clue was me screaming—holding my head and my drooping face. They wanted a better look to determine the extent of the damage.

"Sir, where does it hurt?" the doctor asked. I replied by placing my palm on my neck. He came closer to get a better look and frowned. He lowered the collar of my T-shirt to get a better view. However, it didn't help much, as it still obscured the region.

He turned to a nurse behind him. "Can you help me remove it?"

"Of course." She leaned closer. Her lips were a couple of inches away from my ears.

"Sir, do you mind if I cut your T-shirt?" she whispered.

The T-shirt was the least of my concerns. She could take it off me, but to do so, she would have to prop my body in a sitting position, and she didn't want to move my head.

Without hesitation, I nodded as I could not say yes. Momentarily, I could hear the snap of a scissor, and I felt the cold blade gently slide through my torso. I could breathe better, but the pain in my head wasn't subsiding. I was still screaming in pain. I felt a bright beam of a tiny flashlight aimed at my eyes, shifting from one eye to the other.

I heard a nurse's voice. "What does it look like?"

"No dilation," a male voice answered.

"What do you think, doctor?"

There was a silence for a few seconds as the doctor decided on the next action plan. I screamed again. He looked at my pained face.

"Let's give him morphine," he finally said.

Momentarily, I felt a prick in my left arm and cold liquid flowing through my veins. The pain started to subside but wasn't completely gone; in fact, after a few minutes of relief, it was slowly increasing. After a few minutes, I began to scream again. That's when they gave me a second dose of morphine. That was the last thing I remember happening in the emergency room. I must have passed out, as the next thing I remember was waking up in a bed in the ICU. I heard the familiar sound of the machines beeping as they monitored my vitals.

I heard a melodious voice. "There you are." I blinked at the blurry shape of a human. Then, an image of a kindly nurse came into focus. Her face had sharp features, and her blond hair was tightly tied in a small ponytail. She was wearing blue scrubs with pastel patterns.

"How are you?" she asked me, but, turning to someone else, said. "He's awake."

I turned to see my wife's smiling face. (Or was it a look of relief?) Her eyes were puffy.

She smiled feebly with a relieved look as she gently placed a palm on my forehead. I can only imagine now what must have gone through her mind. I nodded with a feeble smile. Thankfully, the throbbing in my head was gone, but I still felt dizzy and disoriented.

It will be alright, I wanted to say. However, I was too absorbed in my sorrow at that moment. I was well aware of my TBI, but I wasn't aware of the extent of the damage. I didn't realize how permanent it would be. I must have thought it to be a temporary setback and that it would end soon. Now, I realize how life-altering it can be.

In fact, I thought I'd stay in the hospital only for a few days, a maximum of a week. I had already started planning what I would do when I returned and returned to my regular life.

Boy! How wrong was I?

Later, she narrated her harrowing experience in the emergency room.

While she anxiously waited outside for any news, the emergency nurse approached her with a concerned expression.

"How is he doing?" my wife asked her, panicked.

"We don't know yet," the nurse replied.

"What do you mean? He had a stroke, right?"

The nurse nodded. "Yes, we know that."

"So? How bad is it?"

"We don't know. He was in severe pain. We have stabilized him. However, we'll know more about the injury's severity and location once we do an MRI scan. We have taken him for one."

She then looked at my wife with a concerned look. She gently placed her hand on my wife's forearm. Her voice softened. "Do you have any relatives here?"

My wife blinked, looking confused. "Huh?" *What a strange thing to ask! Why is she asking me that?* she thought. "Why?" she said aloud.

"You should call them over."

"W-why?" she stammered. She was alarmed now. This wasn't sounding good.

Yes, we had a big family, but they all were in India. We had no immediate relatives in the U.S. For them to come from India, it would at least take them thirty-six hours. Also, there was a matter of visas. Fortunately, my parents and my in-laws had them. However, not everyone else. There are so many logistical obstacles to overcome. There's a vast difference between taking a domestic flight and flying internationally.

Think of what you'd do if you had your loved ones living abroad.

The nurse looked very uncomfortable when she delivered the news. "Well," she said. "Yes, he's stable now; however, we don't know if he'll make it until we look at the MRI results. Right now, we give him a fifty-fifty chance of survival."

"H-huh." My wife went numb. She heard the nurse's lips moving and understood what she was saying but was unable to process the information. She had begun her day like any other ordinary day, and, in a few hours, her world had turned upside-down.

She had a few cousins and distant relatives in the U.S., but they didn't reside in California. Besides, since India is about twelve hours away, by the time they could come, it would be at least thirty-six hours (if not more).

She was too young to endure this tragedy. She had an infant and a ten-year-old daughter, and she had much to look forward to in life.

So, if I were to die, they would only be able to be there for a widow and two orphans.

* * *

First few days

We are the only ones in the U.S.: my wife, who was thirty-four then, my ten-year-old daughter, and my eighteen-month-old son. Just like for the birth of my daughter—ten years ago, my mother-in-law flew from Mumbai to help my wife when my son was born.

Soon after his birth, my parents arrived. The joy on their faces when they saw him for the first time was infectious. On my insistence, my mother stayed back for a year while my father returned to India. He came back to accompany my mother back. After returning to Mumbai, they flew to Bengaluru (where they resided after they retired). They had lived their working life in Mumbai and had moved to Bengaluru to enjoy their retirement. Just when settling back into the routines of regular life, they got a distressing call from my wife. They had to fly back to the U.S. (via Mumbai).

Even my in-laws had booked their tickets to catch the next flight. However, my wife had suggested they come later after my parents had left—kind of a relay. Besides having moral support, she would need all the help.

Fortunately, all of them had their visas; otherwise, there would have been an additional delay of a few more days.

To add to their woes, when they arrived, my parents were interrogated extensively by the immigration authority.

"You just left the country. Why did you come back so soon?"

"It was an emergency."

"What sort of emergency?"

"Our son has had a stroke. He's hospitalized."

"You stayed for almost a year. How long are you planning to stay this time?"

"However long we have to."

I can only imagine what they must have gone through—the emotional turmoil of their son lying in a hospital and then having to explain. Fortunately, they were granted entry to the U.S.

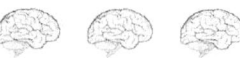

One day, soon after my stroke, when I was in the ICU, two residents came by. They appeared to be students under training. They wore blue scrubs. One of them gently held me and propped me up. Unsteadily, I sat up. My head was pounding. I felt that it was being put through a grinder. The room began to spin. My upper torso began to fall sideways on the bed. The resident who had propped me up caught me from falling by holding my left shoulder while the other held me by my right arm.

"Steady," he said. "Get your bearings."

I looked at him and shook my head. "I can't," I mouthed.

He saw the terror in my eyes. "Don't be afraid." He tightened his grip on my arm. "I'm holding you; I won't let go of you."

His reassurance wasn't helping me. I was in a lot of pain but was in no position to complain. They already knew my state, so they must be doing the right thing.

While one of the residents held me steady, the other resident produced a small hand-held mirror. *What's he doing?* I felt the anger rise in me. *This is no time to look at how I appear.* I looked at him incredulously. It was apparent to him that I was annoyed.

He smiled. "Just look at yourself." He probably was used to such reactions.

Gingerly, I studied my reflection. What I saw shocked me to my core. *Who is this?* A grotesque stranger was looking back at me. One side of his face had drooped—the eyes, the eyebrows, and the lips. I moaned in agony. I was unrecognizable. I looked away. Hesitantly, I peered back at my reflection again, hoping for a miracle to improve my appearance—no such instant gratification.

Ever since then, I've always wondered why this was done. I am not a doctor, but this is my theory. I suspect that they did it on purpose. They must have seen my drooping face. Hence, as a quick fix, my brain must have self-corrected by making me see how I appeared. Time was of the essence. This could have only been possible in a few days after the injury. My brain must have fired the right signals to my facial muscles.

Even after a few years, whenever I visited a specialist, he would ask me to smile. I would always wonder why he asked me to do so; what was he looking for? Now I know why. He must be checking for any degradation in my facial expressions.

After all, our face is the primary mode of communication. Through its expression, it conveys how we feel without having to speak. Without us realizing it, our brain sends the proper signal to various organs. They all work in unison to express our feelings: *smile (turn your lips upward)—decide on what you want to convey: a grin, a toothy smile, a smirk, a glee, and so on, frown—are you thinking or are you concentrating? Be angry—are you annoyed, irritated, or are you mad? Be scared—are you terrified? Be surprised—mildly or astonished?* etc.

I still didn't know what type of stroke I had and in what region. So, I asked the doctor. He started explaining to me: his lips were moving, and words were coming out of his mouth and falling on my ears, but it was of little help. It was all Greek to me. Soon, I was overwhelmed by absorbing all the medical jargon.

I turned to my wife. "Do you understand any of it?"

She shook her head.

The doctor looked at us and smiled. "Tell you what," he said, "I'll send you some material on it."

I nodded. "Okay."

Soon, a nurse came over, holding a few papers. "The doctor asked me to give you this."

"Thank you," my wife said as she took them from her. She scanned them before handing them over to me.

"Why don't you read them to me aloud?" I still couldn't see very clearly. She began to read aloud, but it didn't help much to better understand the symptoms. I was unable to process all the information .

She noticed my fatigue. "Why don't you try getting some rest now?"

So, we decided to go through it later. Soon, we went through the material again, with her narrating to me—more slowly this time, looking up every now and then to look at my face to determine if I had absorbed it or not. Thankfully, I still had my mental faculties intact. The stroke hadn't impacted them. My brain was able to absorb the information.

When she was done reading the material, she asked, "Did you get it?"

I nodded. "Most of it."

Soon, she left, as she had to go back to our house to attend to our children, and I was all alone with my thoughts. There was too much information compressed in a little time. I began to process it. The analytical side of my brain kicked in.

In technical terms, I had an AVM of the Pons area. It is one of the worst kinds of stroke, with a very low survival rate. I guess I'm a freak relic. With the kind of TBI I suffered, the body shuts down significant organs. Hence, the rate of survival is meager.

Here's a brief description from the web:

> A pontine arteriovenous malformation (AVM) is a rare vascular lesion that occurs in the pons, a part of the brain. AVMs are abnormal connections between arteries and veins that bypass the capillaries, the smallest blood vessels connecting the two. This abnormal connection can cause high-pressure arterial blood to flow directly into veins that aren't used to it, leading to bleeding into the brain.
>
> Pontine AVMs are difficult to treat because of their location and surgical and endovascular access challenges.

To complicate things further, my brain was swollen and was now pressing at the walls of my skull. The doctors were worried. Their primary concern now was to subside the swelling naturally. They didn't want to operate on me to ease the pressure. They prescribed prednisone (a steroid) to lessen my swelling. Taken for a short duration, prednisone can do wonders. However, it can be a devastating drug if consumed for an extended period. Fortunately, it did the trick with a few doses. To my doctors' relief, the swelling subsided within a few days. My brain was back to its regular size, albeit not recovered. It still had a long journey ahead.

Even now, when I tell someone that I had an AVM of the Pons, depending on their medical background, they are either surprised to see how I survived it or nod their heads in sympathy, not realizing how serious I was. As the years have passed, I've become used to various reactions—from an astonished look to a sympathetic nod. If I were in their shoes, I would be in the latter category since I am not a medical professional.

Shifted in the general room

* * *

After three days in the ICU, I was shifted to a regular hospital room. I was stable but not out of danger. The severity of the damage had not yet registered. I still was under the impression—more like delusion—that I would be discharged within a few days and go back to my regular life. Boy, was I wrong! In addition to a prolonged stay, I had no clue about the hurdles I had to overcome. All I knew was I had a stroke, and they had 'fixed' it. To me, to be out of the ICU was a sign of progress. Soon, I would leave my hospital room and go home. So, yes, moving into a hospital room from the ICU was a step forward.

After settling in my room, the doctors came to assess me. A tall, bespectacled doctor sat next to my bed. He had a receding hairline and dark circles below his eyes. *Lack of sleep?*

"How are you feeling?" he asked in a concerned voice.

"Fine," I replied.

"How are you feeling?" he asked again, louder this time. *Didn't he hear me?*

"Fine," I repeated, nodding this time.

He looked at my wife and raised his eyebrows. "Why don't you try?"

Try what? Didn't he hear me? What's going on? Why is he looking at me like that? Why is he asking her to try?

She looked at me and said, "He's asking how you feel?" I was getting annoyed by now. *Couldn't they hear me?*

"F.i.n.e." I enunciated each word for their benefit, raising my voice. They looked at each other. I detected an unsaid communication between them. Their concerned expression told me that they didn't understand. I was alarmed. I repeated myself, but this time for my benefit.

"Fffff." My eyes widened with shock. I wanted to say fine, but the words were not right. I didn't realize I was saying 'fine' in my head. My mind lucidly spoke what I wanted to say, but my tongue was refusing to cooperate. It felt like being weighed down.

"Fffff," I repeated, but I coupled it with a thumbs-up sign with my left hand this time. My wife's expression changed from a concerned look to an enlightened one. She understood what I was saying.

"He's saying 'fine'," my wife relayed to the doctor.

Slowly, as the realization dawned on me, my expression changed from annoyed to shocked. *This is not happening. This is just a bad dream. Soon, you'll wake up, and everything will go back to normal.* But it wasn't a bad dream. This was a nightmare in my life.

In addition to my right side completely frozen, I had lost my speech. The doctors could not understand my blabbering. My wife was the only person who could make little sense of what I wanted to communicate. When the doctor asked me any questions, although I tried to respond, I would lift my left hand and yell loudly. My wife then would make a feeble attempt to understand me. It was a shot in the dark. Sometimes, she'd get me; many times, she wouldn't. She would tell the doctors what I meant while constantly looking at me. I then would shake my head or nod. We would play a game of charades, where she had to decipher what I meant. The brain-to-tongue connection was damaged. My brain would hear the question I was asked and know how to respond. However, the words would fail me. They would refuse to come out of my mouth. Thinking clearly about what I wanted to communicate but not being able to convert my thoughts into coherent words was highly frustrating. I felt trapped in my thoughts.

As days progressed, I had devised a strategy to communicate. My speech was slowly returning; however, it had not fully recovered. Mostly, I would either be met with confused looks, 'excuse me's, 'say that again's, or any such variants. I would immediately realize that the opposite person didn't understand me. I then would spell out each word of the sentence. Yes, it was slow and frustrating, but I had no choice. It was the only way to communicate.

Also, to make matters worse, my right side was frozen, so I was not able to write.

When I returned home, I had to practice writing again. Holding the pencil and tracing the words was a challenging task. My hearing also had been affected. I constantly had a buzzing noise in one ear. I could hear from my left ear, but the right was faint. The ENT specialist examined me at the hospital and declared that there wasn't any physical damage. He suggested using a hearing device, but I vehemently resisted. I didn't want any external devices to assist me. I was too young for that.

My vision, too, had been impacted. I would see two of each object a few feet apart. The doctor gave me special glasses to wear, with one side blacked out. I called them 'pirate-glasses.'

> After I returned home, my rehab doctor, Dr. Adams, recommended that I see Dr. Ikeda for vision therapy. He helped me a lot by making me do various visual exercises to improve my vision.

Over time, my vision has improved a lot. Would I call it perfect? No, but much better. The only difference is that I wear reading glasses now. But Dr. Ikeda has informed me that it's very common among folks over forty. Now I keep multiple pairs: on my desk, on a computer, on my sofa in my family room, in my car, etc.

My body was (and still isn't) able to regulate temperature. On my right, I could not distinguish between hot and cold. One-half of my body would correctly measure how hot (or cold) the sensation was. However, the other half couldn't.

Even now, when I have to feel the temperature of something, I use my left hand. It is trivial to someone who doesn't have this issue. However, a simple task such as touching someone's forehead to see if they are running a fever, or determining how hot (or cold) the food is, becomes a challenge. So, I have made such very minor adjustments to live an extraordinary life. I don't even think about it.

When I was in the hospital, I was not able to chew solid food. The doctors feared that I would bite my tongue. Their fears were not misplaced. Even while chewing soft food, I had bitten my tongue innumerable times.

Also, and I was not aware of it, I sometimes drooled. My wife would gently place a tissue in my left hand (our unspoken communication method).

One day, when I was in my bed, I heard footsteps entering my room.

"Knock-knock," the sing-song voice of a therapist said as she entered my room one day.

She was carrying a box with her: a blue-colored square box with a picture of a yellow-colored vertical checkered board with Connect Four written in large letters. She placed the box on my bed and proceeded to open it.

"Have you ever played it before?" she said as she started to assemble the board.

I shook my head.

"It's very easy. It's just like checkers but vertical. Have you played checkers before?"

I nodded.

"Good," she exclaimed as she explained the game's rules. "Got it?" she finally asked.

"Yes," I replied.

We then played a few games for about fifteen minutes. I won all of them. (I suspect she let me win). I now realize that it was not merely a game. It was an exercise to check my dexterity, coordination, cognition, problem-solving skills, etc., to see if I could differentiate between the black and red-colored chips, lift them between my fingers, analyze the pieces already on the gameboard, and insert them in the right slot.

"Very good," she finally exclaimed. She dismantled the board, placed them in the box, and closed it.

"Let's move on," she declared.

She shoved her hands in her pocket, produced flashcards, took one from the pile, and thrust it in front of me. I narrowed my eyes to focus on the image. It had a drawing of an object.

"What is this?" she asked.

"A beach ball."

"Great." She thrust the next card, "This?"

"I recognize the object but don't know what it's called. It falls off trees."

"That's right, it's called an acorn."

She continued to show me around a dozen cards, one after another. I had to identify the object I was seeing. It was a cognitive test. She wanted to see if the stroke had impacted my ability to recognize objects. Fortunately, it hadn't and still hasn't. My memory is intact.

If I had to sum up its effect, I would describe it in computer terms so I could understand it.

My body was going through a reboot. The motherboard was being restarted. The CPU was being initialized, and, soon, it would be loaded with memories. However, the hardware was malfunctioning, and it couldn't be replaced. The CPU had to issue the correct commands for the parts to work again. Soon, the CPU would find out the commands it was issuing were not working. The hardware was not responding correctly. It would have to reprogram itself to issue new instructions that would travel new paths.

Things were cloudy and dismal then, but I was confident they would improve. At night, in solitude, I asked a simple question: "Why me?" The answer was always, "Why not?"

The following morning, when the doctors made their usual rounds to check on me, they informed me that I had to undergo an embolization. *Embo what?* I thought, as I had never heard the word and didn't know what it meant; I just nodded as if I understood.

However, there was a problem. The hospital I was in didn't perform the surgery, and I was to be transferred to USC.

Minoo waiting outside in ICU

When I was in the ICU, I was unaware of ongoings outside. Since none of our relatives resided in California, all my friends—and I still consider them that way— are like my family. I have known some of them since 1989, when I landed in New York. In fact, as one friend pointed out, I have known them for over half of my lifespan on this earth so far. When I first met them, they were all bachelors. I was the only married one with a child. Needless to say, my daughter was thoroughly pampered by her U.S. uncles. Back then, we all were starting our lives in a new country. They all are married now and have adult children. So, yes, they are like my family.

I now realize how important it was to have them give moral support. Not only that, but other trivial things were magnified—food, picking up my daughter from her school, etc.

> Dear reader, all these minor tasks you may take for granted would become an unachievable uphill battle if you had to do them all yourself.

My wife was in the waiting area, surrounded by friends during the day. As the day turned to evening, the ICU waiting room slowly started to get emptier. Eventually, she and a few of our friends were the only ones remaining. The door to the ICU area swung open. A stoutly built nurse, who appeared to be in her fifties, walked in. Her eyes fell upon my wife. She hurried towards her.

"Mrs. Aithal?"

"Yes," my wife answered as she got up. "How is he?"

"He's stable. Resting. He just had his meals. The doctors visited him earlier, and they will be revisiting him." She looked at my wife's tired face. "You should go home and get some rest."

My wife heard the nurse's words but could not process it. She could not imagine leaving me and going home. Back in India, the waiting area would be teeming with family members. She would not have to worry about afore mentioned trivial things like food, picking up my daughter, etc. However, things were very different here. Besides, my friends had to take care of their own daily lives: going to the office, taking care of their children, going grocery shopping, etc. The other thing about Los Angeles is that it is a vast city spread out for miles with notorious traffic. Many of my friends lived far away. It would take them some time to get home. Unlike Mumbai, L.A. is a city with very poor public transportation.

My wife's eyes began to well. "I can't—no, won't—do that. I won't leave him alone."

The nurse saw the resolve in my wife's eyes. Her expression softened, and she gently touched her folded arms. "I understand your sentiment, dear. But you'll be all alone in this deserted room." She waved her hands around.

My wife looked around the quiet room with empty chairs. Fear spread on her face. How would she spend the entire night all by herself?

My friends promptly came to her rescue. "Don't worry. We are here. We'll take turns," one of them reassured her. They took turns (sort of a relay) accompanying her to ensure she was never alone.

The ICU is a sad place. However, the patients there have no clue about what's going on in the waiting area. Sure, it's full of loved ones during the day, but as the night falls, it gets deserted. The dark cloud that hangs around during the day gets gloomier at night. If moral support is not given, it's very easy to slide into depression. It's a place of hopelessness. Besides being there for me, she had to worry about several things: our children, doing the paperwork, talking to the doctors, etc.

I shudder when I look back and think about it.

The following morning, they wheeled me for an MRI again. I was conscious this time. From my bed, lying, all I could see were the blue walls of a wide passageway and bright white ceiling lights passing by as the bed moved forward, strips of white rhythmically passing, interrupted by the blue ceiling, until the next light appeared. They reminded me of yellow road dividers on a dark highway. Occasionally, I'd hear the beeping sound of a monitor—a low chattering as we passed a nurses' station.

Eventually, the white lights slowed as we stopped in front of a steel-gray elevator. The nurse pressed the button and looked at the numbers above the doors. After a while, the doors slid open, and she maneuvered my bed deftly. There were a few others in the elevator: looking up, looking down, looking straight, trying desperately not to stare in my direction. However, I knew they would curiously steal a glance when I was wheeled out and thank their stars that they were not in the bed. It's a natural feeling. We all do it. I know I would do the same if I were in their shoes.

> Dear reader, it's akin to the 'looky-loo' syndrome in a car crash. We all do that. We curse others, holding up the traffic to have a better look. But when it's our turn, we do the same.

I was wheeled into a vast room. An enormous tubular steel machine lay vertically in the center, and a narrow steel bed jutted out of it like a tongue emerging from an open mouth.

On the far side of the room, a glass window divided a smaller room. It housed various screens for monitoring activity.

A door on its side opened, and a technician in his blue scrubs appeared to assist the nurse.

They gently transferred me to the narrow bed that would slide me into the tube. As they were transferring me, the room began to spin. I started to experience a warm sensation at the base of my neck. My head started to pound. I wanted them to lift my head but could not speak as I had lost my speech. Also, I couldn't signal them by moving my head, as that would cause more pain. To make things more challenging, my right side was frozen. I was trapped. I didn't know what to do. So, desperately, I grabbed at the last straw and tried one thing I could. I slowly lifted my left hand and made a circular motion, trying to tell them the room was spinning. I then lowered my hand and brought it under my neck to indicate that my head needed to be lifted.

They looked at each other in confusion.

"Fan? Are you warm?" the nurse asked.

"No," I mouthed. I lifted my hand once again to make the same motion.

"Spinning?"

"Yes!" I mouthed. I then moved my hand to my neck.

"Ah! Lift, you want us to lift your head."

Once again, I mouthed a yes.

They quickly placed a pillow below my neck. The technician looked at me quizzically, "Okay?"

I gave him a thumbs-up.

He nodded and pressed a button on the panel. The bed I was in gently slid into the narrow tube. He then went to the small room that separated the machine and the control panel. He could monitor the machine through a glass panel. My head was only a few inches away from the tube's ceiling. Its side walls were also a couple of inches away from my shoulders. My feet were the only part of my body that was out; the monstrous MRI machine now encapsulated the rest of my body.

"Are you okay?" crackled a voice above me. It was the technician.

Am I okay? What a funny thing to ask, I thought. *No, I'm not okay.* I wanted to scream, but I just grunted. After all, he was doing his job and was trying to make me as comfortable as possible.

"Okay, the whole procedure should last about forty minutes. You'll hear a lot of knocking, but don't worry. It's normal. Try to stay still. Please don't move your head; otherwise, we will have to redo it. Do you want some music?"

What? Music? I was stunned. I shook my head very weakly. I didn't have the strength to shake it more vigorously.

"Okay. Here we go."

The machine must be equipped with a camera.

I lay there in eerie silence for a few seconds, waiting for something to happen. Soon, I was surrounded by a buzzing sound as the large magnets rotated in the tube, followed by an incessant and rhythmic knocking on its circular walls as though many people were knocking on the other side of the tube.

After a grueling—what felt like an eternity, the sound stopped.

I heard his voice over the speaker. "Okay, great! We are done. You did well."

I then heard a door open, followed by approaching footsteps. A low hum slid me out of the dreaded tube. Momentarily, the nurse appeared back, shifted me to my bed, and rolled me back to the ICU.

I was in the ICU for three days.

USC

USC Hospital (Keck Medicine of USC) is one of the best hospitals in the country. It has consistently been ranked among the top three in L.A. and the top ten in California.

Soon, they transferred me to USC Hospital. By now, I was familiar with the environment of lying flat on a gurney at the back of the ambulance while sirens blared. Lying down, I could only imagine the ambulance speeding forward and the cars hurriedly moving aside when they heard the siren's blare. From where I was, I could only see the ceiling and hear radio chatter. I moved my head to take in the surroundings. Oxygen tanks, makeshift IVs hanging off shelves, first-aid kits with a bright red plus, and many other items. Transparent, plastic cubbyholes on the walls displayed various assortments of medicine, each clearly labeled to indicate what it contained. I tilted my head a little to see the driver's cabin. All I could see were the back of two heads bobbing now and then. Occasionally, one of the paramedic's heads would turn around to check on me. The consistent blare of the siren had become less frequent now that we were on the freeway. However, I had witnessed—in the past—that they would drive on the shoulder of the freeway where other vehicles were not permitted to drive.

How I wish I were in a sitting position, witnessing the notorious traffic of L.A. making way for us. After about an hour's drive north, we reached our destination. I was immediately wheeled to a room housing one bed. I thanked my stars for not having to share the room with another patient. Like many, I've always found hospitals depressing to my spirits. I didn't want to be dragged down any further by seeing another human being who wasn't well. After all, hospitals are not a happy place. In my opinion, the only exceptions are the maternity wards, where a newborn comes into the world, and the relatives are joyous in giving her or him a better future.

The nurse came by to take my vitals. I asked her when the procedure would take place. She ignored my question, continuing to take my vitals. So, I asked her again.

Finally, she shrugged her shoulders. "I don't know. Soon."

That helps me a lot, I thought sarcastically. She wasn't being very informative.

"What do you mean 'I don't know?' When will they take me in?"

She continued to concentrate on the blood pressure monitor. She raised her index finger. "One moment, please," she mouthed as she looked at the dial, pumping vigorously to inflate my armband.

When she was done, she jotted down my numbers, deflated the armband, and looked at me. "Go ahead," she said.

"We were talking about when I would be taken, and you said you didn't know. I was wondering why."

"Right," she said.

"So, why? Why don't you know?"

"That's because you are not a direct patient," she said.

"Huh?" I was confused. Her reply wasn't helping me.

She saw my confused expression. "Since you are not our direct patient, in other words, you were not directly admitted here but transferred from another hospital for a procedure, you will be given lower priority. Our direct patients will be serviced first," she explained.

That didn't sound good. I didn't even know how many people were ahead of me.

"How long will I have to wait? Are there many patients ahead of me?"

"There are a few, But thankfully, you are now in the queue."

"Good. Any idea how long I will have to wait?"

"No. Sorry. Maybe for a day or two." She sounded uncertain. "You'd better eat well today."

I made a face. "Ugh." I was not looking forward to another hospital tray of liquid food consisting of Jellos and juices.

She looked at me, her expression now a little more confident. "You can't consume any food on the day of the procedure."

Her words affected my stomach. Suddenly, it started to grumble in protest. I was hungry now, and the hospital food (which I used to hate) started sounding yummy.

"Nothing?"

"Nothing," she confirmed, shaking her head.

"Not even water?"

"Not even water."

I was crestfallen. Of course, I had fasted for a day, but that was voluntary. This was a forced situation.

> Dear reader, I'm sure you have experienced a similar situation. Once you are forbidden from doing something, that thought is magnified and constantly plays in your mind. You want to do it more now that you have been told no.

This didn't sound good.

"What do I do if I get thirsty?"

"You can use ice cubes to wet your lips," she said, "But *only* to wet your lips. You are not allowed to put them in your mouth," she warned.

Suddenly, I felt thirsty, as if my mouth was parched. Subconsciously, I wet my lips with the saliva on my tongue.

"So, if I'm the first person taken in the morning, it won't matter, right?" I looked at her hopefully.

She nodded. "Right. But doubtful. As I told you just now, a few patients are ahead of you. Hence, your turn will most likely come towards the end of the day. Do you understand?"

I nodded gloomily.

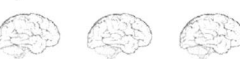

The following day, I stayed hungry and thirsty, awaiting my turn. I tried to divert my mind from the dryness in my mouth and hunger pangs. Occasionally, the nurse would appear, holding a bowl of ice cubes. She would then proceed to rub them gently on my parched lips.

I would jut out my tongue, and she would move her hand away.

"No, no. Just your lips."

I then would roll my tongue over my lips, trying desperately to collect whatever residues of dew I could.

The day turned into the evening and then night, yet I wasn't called. Finally, the evening nurse came by to inform me that I would have to wait until the next day. My heart sank. How was I supposed to stay hungry through the night? How was I supposed to stay hungry and thirsty for over twelve hours?

"Can I eat?" I begged in a panicked voice.

She nodded. "Yes, of course. I'll be right back."

She left the room and returned with a hospital tray. Hungrily, I looked at it. It contained a few assortments of colorful Jellos and juice. Usually, I'd look at hospital food with disgust, but it never seemed so attractive to me.

Fortunately, the following day, I was taken in for the procedure late in the evening. I was the last patient for the day. Although I had already endured hunger and thirst for another day, I was relieved it was the previous day. I would not have to stay hungry for one more day.

I was wheeled into the room and gently transferred to the operating bed. The room was cold. As I lay there, my vision was limited to the ceiling. I turned my head. A young man was resting on a table in a corner. He was Dr. Arun Amar. He would be performing the procedure.

> He was under training then and is now the director of endovascular neurosurgery, chief of neurosurgery, stroke director, and neurotrauma liaison.

A smiling face slid into my vision. "Hello, Mr Aithal. My name is (I forget his name.) I'm an anesthesiologist. I will administer the proper dose to ensure the procedure goes smoothly. Do you have any questions?"

I shook my head.

"Good," he said, smiling as he nodded. "Here we go." He covered my face with a plastic mask and asked me to count backward from ten. I must have counted to seven before the room went blank. I was unconscious.

Since I didn't know much about the procedure, I recently looked it up and was amazed to read what I found. I don't want to bore you with the gory details, so here's a summary:

> *During the procedure, a neuro-interventional surgeon inserts a catheter into a blood vessel, usually*

> *in the groin, and threads it to the AVM using X-rays. They then inject a substance or device, such as medical glue, metal coils, or plugs, to block blood flow to the AVM.*

I was in my room the next time I opened my eyes. It was dark. Slowly, I turned my head to see Dr. Arun Amar sleeping on the sofa. Hearing me making tiny sounds as I shuffled in my bed, he opened his eyes. A look of relief spread across his face. "He's okay," he said to someone. I turned my head to see my wife. Her face was covered with mixed emotions of relief and sadness.

Later, I found out that the procedure was not successful. They had to pull out because my veins were too tiny, and, understandably, they didn't want to take any chances.

After the embolization process, I felt that my brain had rebooted again. Strange and unconnected thoughts started to swirl, and I felt caught at sea in a thunderstorm.

Chapter 2

At USC after the embolization

I STAYED AT THE USC hospital for a few days before I was moved back to Long Beach Memorial. It was a stay, not an out-of-choice one. Was Long Beach Memorial fully occupied, I wondered. However, I was wrong in my assumption. They had plenty of empty beds, but they were understaffed. So, I patiently waited (not that I had a choice) to be called back.

Waiting was the hardest part. Time moved at a snail's pace. Moreover, since I was not their direct patient, there were no therapy sessions. I would be doing all that upon my return. All I could do was bide my time, and I hope I will be quickly transferred. I was getting restless and wanted to start my sessions. I remembered what the doctors had told me: The first year is crucial for your recovery.

Every day passed was a day lost towards the path of my recovery. Time was passing by, and I could do nothing about it.

I was still on a soft diet. One day, a therapist came to examine me to see if I was ready for solid food. She had an oval face with expressive eyes. She had tied her curly hair into a tight bun. She appeared to be a trainee in her early twenties.

She sat beside me on my bed and helped me prop up in a sitting position. She put a soft pillow behind me to make me comfortable.

"Is this okay?" she asked, and I noticed the dimples on her cheek.

I nodded.

"Good, now let's have a look," she said, smiling. "Open your mouth."

"Aaaa." I obeyed her, hoping that the result she was looking for was in my favor.

She peeled a boiled egg, cut it into small pieces, and gently placed one of the tiniest pieces in my mouth.

"Close, please," she said as she closed my mouth, pushing her index finger on my chin. I obeyed her, feeling the softness of the boiled egg. My mouth felt weird having solid food after many days.

"Start chewing," she instructed.

She moved her jaw from side to side to show me what she wanted me to do. I mimicked her.

"Chew, chew, chews...grind, grind, grind," she said as she exaggeratedly chomped.

Gingerly and carefully, I began to chew, ensuring my tongue would not be crushed between my teeth.

> Dear reader, it frequently occurred in the beginning years. I have inadvertently crushed

my tongue in between my teeth. Several times, I've bitten so hard that it has been out of commission for a while, further slurring my speech. Fortunately, it hasn't happened to me in years.

She was closely observing my mouth movements.

After a little while, she said, "Very good. Now, open your mouth wide."

She pulled a tiny flashlight from her pocket, switched it on, and beamed it into my mouth. She peeked in. Her eyebrows furrowed. "Hmm."

I wondered what she was seeing. I raised my eyebrows to indicate, 'What?'

"Well, Mr. Aithal, you still aren't ready," she said as she switched it off and placed it back in her pocket.

Panicked, I raised my eyebrows again; *why?*

"You are chewing your food only on one side, and that too not very confidently. Look at this."

She proceeded to use a plastic spoon to scoop out half-chewed food and dump it in a steel tray. The yellow and white of the egg mixed with my saliva had become a gooey mess—something that had been so attractive just a few seconds ago. Not only that, it had lost its shape and definition—a solid piece of object that now looked hideous and unrecognizable.

"You are unable to chew even semi-soft food." She placed the spoon—dripping with a now unattractive blob—on the tray. She then turned to me and looked into my eyes.

"If you chew solid foods, you might inadvertently chew your tongue. I'm sorry. You have to go back on a soft diet for a few more days."

I closed my eyes. I was not looking forward to another liquid diet.

"Don't worry," she said when she saw my disappointed look. "It'll come back. You'll once again be able to enjoy food."

I was very disappointed then, but now I realize she was right. I had chewed my tongue very frequently several times during the early days after they switched me to solid food. The frequency has lessened—and ultimately stopped.

Also, in the initial days after the stroke onset, I had lost my sense of taste. I no longer enjoyed food. I was eating to live instead of living to eat. After a few days, the first type of food I could taste was sweets. I would crave them.

I guess that's why I immensely enjoy sweets—even now.

I spent a few more days there. They would wheel me to a huge window that overlooked the activities on the ground to lift my gloomy spirits. That's when I realized I was on the second (or third) floor.

The nursing staff came by regularly to take my vitals, blood, etc. But thankfully, I wasn't subjected to the torture of going into an MRI machine.

Also, because of the distance and the heavy traffic, it was a logistical nightmare for my wife to visit me several times a day. When I was at Long Beach Memorial, she could conveniently make several trips in a single day. However, here, she could *only* make one trip. My father stayed with me for the length of my stay there.

I just waited to be called back.

Eventually, the call came. I was overjoyed. Once again, I was in an ambulance's now familiar rear compartment, eagerly looking forward to starting my therapy sessions.

I was kept in a double-occupancy room adjacent to the nurses' station. I suspect this was intentional. They had deemed I needed a constant watch close by so they could instantaneously attend to me in an emergency.

It was a small room with two beds, each separated by a flimsy curtain for privacy, which stopped a few feet above the ground. A small TV was mounted high above in a corner that almost touched the ceiling. A small wash basin was in one corner with a mirror on top. A tiny bulb illuminated the area. Next to it was the door to the shower room. On the right side of my bed was an expansive window overlooking a courtyard with a few benches and small trees. It was designed to lift the spirits of patients.

They shifted me to my bed. I had guard rails on each side to prevent me from rolling down. I looked up. I furrowed my eyebrows in confusion, trying to decipher the object above me. It took me a while to process what I was seeing. A steel rod ran perpendicularly a few feet above me, from my head to toe. A handle hung from it, just above my torso.

"What is this?" I asked, looking at it and raising my eyebrows. By now, my speech was slowly returning. However, it was very thick. The words were jumbled. My brain was speaking the dialog, but my mouth wasn't cooperating.

Moreover, I wasn't very confident in my speech. I restricted myself from talking as little as possible and compensated with facial expressions. However, that, too, was a challenge as I wasn't sure if my brain was sending the proper commands: Smile, frown, raise your eyebrows, and so on. I often found myself spelling the words to communicate what I meant. Also, by now, I had learned to improvise. I would use the combination of my mouth, my facial expressions, and my left hand to convey my thoughts. After all, communication was paramount, irrespective of the tools available at my disposal.

"Oh, this?" the nurse pointed.

I nodded. "Yes."

"It's for you to hold while you heave yourself up," she explained.

"Oh," I mumbled.

I was immediately transported to my past. It took me back to Mumbai's local trains as a young man. The dozens of such handles—rhythmically swaying above the travelers as the train plunged forward—looked exactly like them. The passengers would hold onto them to stop themselves from colliding with the others during rush hours.

It looked out of place. My brain was not geared to see it in this environment. I was used to seeing them on Mumbai trains, but not here. I wrapped my palms around it and pulled it to check its strength. The rod bent slightly but was sturdy enough to hold my weight. As I let go, it swayed back and forth gently.

I wondered how long I would have to depend on it.

"Now, do you need anything else?" her voice brought me back from Mumbai locals.

I shook my head.

"Okay then. Good night," she said as she covered me with a bed sheet. She turned off the lights as she exited.

Back at Long Beach Memorial

A cheerful voice disturbed my slumber. "Good morning."

Slowly and groggily, I opened one of my eyes. I squinted to focus on the clock that hung on the wall. 7:00 A.M. I groaned and shut my eyes again, desperately hoping the nurse with the sing-song voice would take pity on me and let me sleep for another fifteen minutes, but that was not to be.

"Good morning," she repeated, louder this time. She then turned on the lights and opened the curtains to let in the sunlight.

I squeezed my eyes to shield them from the sudden change.

"The therapist will be here soon," she said.

This time, reluctantly, I opened my eyes, and holding the handle, I heaved myself up.

Soon, a young man walked in. "Hi, I'm Charles." He pointed at his nametag.

"Hi, Charlie," I mumbled.

Hearing me abbreviate his name, he grunted and smiled crookedly.

Did I say something wrong? I should have called him by his full name. "Is it okay if I call you Charlie?"

"Well," he said, "I usually don't like being addressed by Charlie, but I'll make an exception in your case."

Phew, I sighed.

He was of Asian descent, with straight jet-black hair and matching eyes. He wore jeans and a blue tee with the Dodgers written in white. He had a thick cream-colored canvas belt with red and blue stripes running along its length casually flung on his shoulder. It was about 2 inches wide and over 50 inches long, with a shiny buckle on one end. It was longer than the regular belt I wore.

"What is that?" I asked, raising my eyebrows and gazing at it (I was getting good at expressing myself without having to speak a lot).

"Oh, this?" He turned his head. "It's a gait belt."

"What is it for?" I asked again, using a combination of my speech and facial expressions.

"It's for both of us. I'll tie it around your waist. Not only will it help me to guide you, but also help me prevent you from falling."

"Oh," I said, as he slipped the belt around my waist.

"Also, it'll protect me from back injuries when I have to shift you from a sitting position to a standing one. All the therapists use them."

"Oh," I said again, as he secured the belt around his waist.

> Dear reader, that was my first introduction to the gait belt. Since then, I've been tethered to a gait belt whenever I've gone for physical therapy. In fact, it's a common sight with many patients performing various physical tasks while they are tethered.
>
> I humbly request you to visit one of these centers to appreciate life. It'll make you look at your success in a different light. Your priorities will change. You will deeply think about the things that were the most important things for you.
>
> Enough of philosophy. Let's get back to my journey.

He looked at me, and raised his eyebrows. "Ready?" he asked.

I nodded nervously. I held the handle dangling above my bed and heaved myself to sit. I then swung my legs to the floor to face him.

"Lift your arms like this," he instructed, lifting his own to his side, making a T.

I mimicked him.

He came close to me and wrapped the belt around my hospital gown. It was a few inches above the usual place to tie a belt. He slid one end through the buckle and tightened it to ensure it was securely fastened. "Tight enough?" he asked.

I nodded.

"Here we go."

He came closer, bent his knees, held the strap at my back, and gently lifted me to the wheelchair beside my bed. He then wheeled me to the washbasin in the corner.

"Ready?" he asked again.

I nodded but wasn't sure what he was doing or what he wanted me to do.

He heaved me up and made me stand in front of the sink, which had a mirror above it. It was the very first time that I was propped up in a standing position after my stroke. It was an effort. I was unsteady. I tightly held on to the edges of the sink to stop the wobbling. I felt my knees were going to buckle under me. My pulse had quickened. I could feel my heart pounding and blood rushing to my brain.

He put one hand on my shoulder to steady me.

I looked at him with terror in my eyes. I shook my head. I wanted to sit back in my wheelchair.

"Don't be afraid. You won't fall. I'm holding you. The wheelchair is right behind you.

What does he want me to do? Does he want me to brush?

"W—what now?" I asked him with a strained voice.

"I want you to lather your face and try to shave."

"Yeah, right." I thought he was joking.

"No, I'm serious."

I looked at him in the mirror with astonishment (we were conversing via the mirror). His earnest expression told me he was not kidding.

What? Are you crazy? I wanted to scream.

My angry expression must have shown that he understood what I was thinking.

"That's right," he said, smiling, "I know you must hate me now, but you'll thank me in the future."

Thank you? I was flabbergasted. I could feel my temper rising as the back of my neck felt warmer. *Calm down. He knows what your condition is. He knows what he's doing.* However, I still wasn't convinced. I looked at my reflection. I didn't need a shave. My father had shaved me the previous day while I was lying in my bed.

> Yes, dear reader, several morning activities were performed on me while I lay in bed. My father would shave me, my wife would brush my teeth and comb my hair, etc.

I protested. "But why? I shaved yesterday. I don't need one today."

"It's not that. You have to practice shaving. Your hand has to get used to the movements of lathering your face and applying the proper amount of pressure on your face so that you don't cut yourself. After all, you don't want to depend on someone else to care for your hygiene for the rest of your life, right?"

I was frustrated then, but looking back, his ruthlessness made me realize how right he was. I can perform all my morning functions without any assistance. Many frustrating instances back then have worked out for me to lead an everyday life (well, as normal as possible).

The biggest mistake I (like most of us who have gone through a TBI) made was to compare myself to what I could have done before my stroke instead of comparing how far I had come since that fateful day.

When I was done lathering my face, my face was a white mess. I looked at Charlie for approval.

"Good job," he encouraged me.

"Yeah, right. I look like a clown."

"No," he said. "Sure, a regular person could do a neater job. However, you're doing a good job as a first-timer with your condition. Now, the razor."

I apprehensively picked it up and ran it under the faucet for a few seconds. I then gingerly brought it to my face.

"Slowly … carefully."

With my tongue, I puffed the left side of my cheek and started to shave while Charlie watched me closely. Every now and then, he would remind me to do it gently and with proper pressure, ensuring I didn't cut myself.

When I was done, he put me back in the bed.

"Very good," he said as he unbuckled my gait belt and flung it over his shoulder. "I'll go tell the nurse for your next task."

He left, and, after a few minutes, the nurse entered.

"Ready?" she asked.

"For?" I asked back.

"Shower."

"Ah," I exclaimed.

She went into the bathroom and came back with a steel wheelchair.

I was bare, devoid of any cushions. As she shifted me in it, I felt the cold steel touching my bare skin.

She wheeled me to the bathroom. She turned on the shower, let the water run for a while until it warmed up, and felt the temperature of the running water. She gently aimed the showerhead towards my hand.

"Is it warm enough?"

How was she to know that I couldn't feel the temperature on my right side? Slowly, I lifted my left hand to touch the running water. Satisfied, I nodded. The warm water falling on my skin felt like heaven.

She then proceeded to spray me for five minutes.

After I had bathed, she changed my gown and combed my hair. I felt anew and invigorated. The act of a shave and shower had lifted my mood. I was ready to tackle the challenges of the day.

She shifted me to my regular wheelchair and wheeled me out of the room to the nurses' station, where I joined a queue of patients on wheelchairs—an assembly line of patients getting ready to be wheeled to the therapy area.

Computer experience

* * *

Soon, Charlie came over to take me to the therapy area. "You look fresh," he observed.

"Thank you," I said. "I feel clean."

"Ready?" he asked as he came behind my wheelchair.

I nodded.

He unlocked my wheelchair and steered it deftly. I could tell that he was used to navigating them through the crowd. It put me at ease. Dear reader, it's not as easy as it looks.

On my way to the therapy room, he started having an innocuous conversation with me. My wife, who had joined us just on our way to the therapy area, was walking beside him.

"What do you do?" I noticed that he didn't say 'what *did you do*'. It was his way of encouraging me to live in the present.

"C-c-computers," I stammered. I was struggling with my words.

"Excuse me?" he leaned forward, bringing his ear closer to my face.

I realized my words were slurring, and he had difficulty deciphering them. So, I wiggled my fingers in front of me like I was typing on an imaginary keyboard.

"Music? You play a piano?"

I shook my head vigorously. Again, I wiggled my fingers.

"C-c-computers."

"Ah, Computer!" he exclaimed.

I nodded.

"That's right," my wife said, "he's a software consultant." She had now become my de facto interpreter. If anyone understood what I was trying to communicate, it was her.

> Dear reader, God forbid you have to be admitted to a hospital. You need a family member to have your back. You are in no condition to think clearly. You need a loved one to make crucial

decisions.

My wife was the one. She watched over me like a guardian angel.

Once, the nurse came by and gave me medication. Soon, the shift changed. The nurse on the new shift read my chart and thought I had not been given the medicines. She was about to double-dose me when my wife stopped her. There have been several such occasions when her intervention has been highly crucial. I was in no condition to express what I was feeling.

Once, when I was sitting in a wheelchair for a very long time, I started to experience significant pain. I began to moan in agony.

My wife immediately called the nurse.

She hurried into my room.

"He needs to lie down for a while," she told the nurse.

"Sorry, ma'am, we are not allowed to do that."

"What? Why?" my wife shouted incredulously.

"The therapists instruct us that he should remain seated."

"That's not acceptable. He is in a lot of pain."

I continued to moan in agony.

"I can see that, but I'm sorry. There's nothing I can do without their approval."

Just then, I moaned a little louder.

My wife looked at me with alarm. "Call the doctors," she finally said, knowing that they would be able to override the therapists' instructions.

"Okay." The nurse left the room to call the doctors.

My wife turned to me, looked at me with concern and helplessness, and held my hand. "The doctors will be here soon." She squeezed my hand to reassure me.

Soon, I was surrounded by a bunch of them. Their primary concern was to check for any clues that I was having another stroke: was my face contorted, showing any signs of drooping, complaining of a headache, my breathing irregular, etc?

"Smile, please."

"Do you feel me touching your leg?"

"Look at the tip of my finger. Follow it as I move my hand without moving your head."

"Do you have any tingling sensation?"

"Do you hear any buzzing sound?"

Once they had determined I was in the clear, they turned to address my issue.

After a brief examination, one of them misdiagnosed me.

"He's depressed," he declared.

"What?" my wife yelled, not believing her ears. "No, he's not."

I would have used a few harsh expletives if I were in her place.

My wife continued: "Can't you see that he is in pain? He needs to be shifted out of this wheelchair and to the bed for a little while."

However, the doctor would disagree; my wife stood her ground. This back-and-forth argument continued for a while. Finally, they made her sign a waiver saying she took full responsibility for the consequences. Only then did they relent and shift me to the bed without administering medication.

Merely leaving a loved one in the care of strangers—no matter how qualified they may be—is not enough. A close family member has to constantly keep an eye on and be fearless in questioning them. After all, they, too, are humans who can make mistakes.

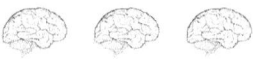

As I entered the massive therapy room, I was awed. In the center, there were many foam-covered blue beds. In one corner, a foam mattress lay on the floor. A patient was lying down on it, and a therapist was instructing him on what to do. It looked so easy when she did it, but the patient was sweating as he struggled to imitate her.

I shuffled my body, getting ready for a bout with the mattress.

However, I was surprised when he wheeled me to the door at the far end.

He pressed on my shoulders to sit back. "Not yet."
Where is he taking me?

I looked around as he wheeled me into the room. It was much smaller. It was devoid of beds, mattresses, or intimidating equipment. Instead, it consisted of items that one used daily.

In one corner, a gas range stood next to a refrigerator. In another corner, a ceramic toilet stood. A desk (without a chair) flushed against the wall in the far corner, adorned with a map. A computer sat on it.

It was jarring to see all of them clubbed together in one room rather than seeing them in their respective rooms. A regular house would have different rooms for each: a kitchen, a bathroom, a home office, etc. To see them clubbed together in a single room was a surreal experience.

A patient held a coffee mug in her hand, taking it from the microwave (above the gas range) and taking a few steps to the nearby table. A therapist, who walked behind and encouraged her, tethered her with a tightly held gait belt. Her face was flushed, and her hand was trembling, trying not to spill the liquid. Even though the table was only a few feet away from the microwave, it was apparent that it was a herculean task for her.

Another patient was practicing sitting on the toilet. He, too, had a gait belt around his waist and was closely monitored by another therapist. The therapist instructed the patient, "Knees over your feet, lift yourself with them and not your back, use your core, don't forget to breathe," etc.

I could tell that it was an effort to do these mundane activities. Both the patients were sweating and concentrating on what they were doing.

> Dear reader, healthy human beings perform such tasks without giving any thought. It has become a muscle memory. However, it becomes an enormous task for anyone whose body has forgotten to do so.

He wheeled me to the desk and slid my wheelchair so that I was in front of the computer. Microsoft Paint was open on the terminal. He gently placed my hand on the mouse.

"Can you move the cursor to select red?"

Easy, I thought. I nodded. I moved the mouse and left-clicked, looking at the screen for the cursor to respond to my action. I frowned. I was confused. The cursor had moved over the red color and stood there still. I looked down and clicked again. Nothing. My heart sank. I was alarmed now. My hand was moving, but my fingers were refusing to obey the command fired by my mind. Being able to operate a computer was everything to me.

My pulse quickened, and I started to sweat profusely. Beads of sweat began to form on my forehead. I was feeling hot, and I panicked.

I tried it again, concentrating harder this time. My tongue slightly jutted out from the corner of my closed mouth. The sweat—that had formed on my forehead—coalesced to run down my nose. I was now looking down at my index finger, desperately willing to respond. However, it refused to cooperate. It stood still—resting on the left-click button, waiting on my command. My brain was repeatedly firing the command, but my finger lay there without any response.

Charlie could sense my frustration. He gently moved my hand from the mouse. "It's okay, we'll try it again. Just give it some time. It'll return."

However, at that moment, I felt my world crumbling around me. Without being able to work on a computer, I was nothing.

For the first time after my stroke, I felt disabled.

Family visit

Soon, Charlie wheeled me back to my room. My mind was still in shock, and a sense of despair engulfed me. I was doomed without access to a computer. The most frustrating thing was that my mind knew what to do, but my body wouldn't cooperate. I felt trapped. I have been through these frustrating instances several times. However, my resolve to get better has landed me where I am today.

I was exhausted. The whole episode had left a bitter taste in my mouth. I started to think of all the tasks I would be unable to do if I could not move my fingers. I began to doubt my abilities. *Will I be able to hold a spoon or a remote? Will I be able to hold any object at all? Will I be able to do a handshake? What if I squeeze too tight? What if I have a glass in my hand that breaks because I held it too tight?*

Thankfully, today I can do these things and many more.

I may sound like a broken record, but I will repeat it: *keep trying, never give up. Soon, when you look back, you'll realize how far you have come. Yes, the journey may be challenging and treacherous sometimes. That is when you lift yourself. Nobody can help you the way you help yourself. If those around you see you are trying, they will be encouraged to help you. I'm not just preaching; I'm narrating my own experience. You may have a very different journey.*

My family entered as I lay in bed, feeling sorry for myself. I was seeing my children for the first time since my stroke. My mother carried my son in her arms. She gently placed him on my bed. Immediately, he crawled forward, sat on my stomach, and started playing with my face. My daughter came close to me. She was smiling, but I could tell that she had been crying. I looked at my parents. They, too, were smiling, but I could see a look of worry on their faces.

Looking at them, a warm and fuzzy feeling engulfed me. Their unsaid love had lifted my low mood. My gloom had disappeared. My spirits were lifted. For a while, I had forgotten about my misfortune a little while ago.

I was dying to hold my son but was too afraid of my coordination. I was worried that I'd injure him. For a long time, even after my return, he would innocently ask me, "When will you be fine?" He wanted me to be normal (like other dads) who played catch with their sons. Although my daughter was old enough to understand the severity of my stroke, she, too, was distraught. It must have been challenging to go through the ruthless teens with an added emotional rollercoaster of one parent not always being there for her.

And my wife has endured so much. I was in the hospital for fifty-three days. I can't imagine coming to a house in the evening when you know your husband is not there. Or suddenly waking up in the middle of the night only to find an empty bed beside you. She has been solely responsible for raising my children in their early years. Many times, she has fulfilled the role of a father. When my son was old enough to play soccer and all the little kids had to practice kicking a ball with their fathers, she was the only mother kicking the ball. Sometimes, I think that it's easier for me than her. Taking care of someone briefly is one thing, but doing it for the rest of one's life is unique.

People always sympathize with the person in the wheelchair but often fail to appreciate the person pushing it.

One needs a partner who constantly pushes you—not just the wheelchair—to do better. Sometimes, things can get rough, but they always get better.

Seeing them lifted my spirits, and I was determined to stop feeling sorry for myself.

> Now, my wife and I are empty-nesters, and we miss the liveliness in the house, but I'm proud to see my children turn into adults with successful lives.

As I've said before, we four are the only Aithals in the U.S. However, I'm fortunate to have many friends whom I consider family. They were all there for us in times of crisis. Yes, they are sensitive to my needs but have never made me feel different.

I consider myself blessed to have such a good family and friends.

The nurse came by and reminded me that I needed to rest before my next therapy. They left, and my wife and I were left alone.

I was too charged up to sleep, but she reminded me that I should get some rest before the next therapy. "Try to sleep." She pulled down the curtains to make the room darker.

I closed my eyes. Soon, I was snoring.

I felt a gentle shake. Slowly, I opened my eyes. The pleasant oval-shaped face of a nurse came into focus. I had never seen her before.

"Hello," she said, smiling. "Good afternoon."

I yawned. "What time is it?"

"Four o'clock," she said, pointing to the clock behind her.

I looked at her. She wore jeans and a tee. She had the now familiar gait belt on her shoulder.

"Afternoon," I mumbled, stretching myself lazily and reaching for the handle to heave myself upright.

"I'm Suzy," she said, pointing at the nametag.

I nodded. "Hi," I said, minimizing myself to speak more words as I was unsure how they would sound.

"What exercise will you make him do?" my wife asked.

"Not exercises," she declared. "Activities."

"Activities?"

"We will be potting a plant."

I was confused. "Huh?"

"I'm not a physical therapist. I'm an occupational therapist. My primary goal is to make you do some daily activities for the dexterity in your hands to return. A physical therapist works on your gross motor skills, whereas an occupational therapist works on fine motor skills. An occupational therapist may make you perform mundane tasks such as playing a video game, typing an email, and more. The idea is to develop dexterity in your fingers, such as holding things and applying the proper amount of pressure. Thankfully, you have not lost the sensation of touch. We just want to retrain your brain to issue the right commands. In addition, a speech therapist will work on your speech. Together, we work on you in tandem to improve your condition."

I nodded. "Oh," I said, now understanding the different types of therapists and their roles. So far, I had only dealt with doctors, nurses, MRI technicians and physical therapists. I now realized how big and complex the machinery was. I started to appreciate the enormity of a mammoth operation to work on improving a single human being.

Besides, I realized that making me perform such tasks would help me with my computer debacle.

"Ready?" she asked me as she grabbed the gait belt from her shoulder.

I nodded.

Deftly, she shifted me to the wheelchair and wheeled me

out. I was surprised when she turned right—the therapy area was on the left. She wheeled me out to the courtyard I had seen earlier through my window.

It had a small gardening area in a corner with all the tools. She stooped in front of a wooden table. It had an empty pot and a small shovel. Next to it was a plastic bag containing potting soil and mulch. A miniature succulent lay next to it.

My job was to plant it in the pot. Having never done it before, I looked at her with raised eyebrows. She immediately understood.

"Take some soil from the bag with the shovel and layer it half full. First, make a base, then hold the succulent while you fill the rest of the pot with the soil around it. Once it stands independently, pat the soil around it to tighten it. Easy."

For you.

I proceeded to pot the plant.

"Excellent job," she said at the end.

However, I know she was lying. The plant stood crooked. There was not enough soil to hold it straight.

Next, she handed me a small watering can that was half filled. "Water it," she instructed.

After I had poured some water, she replaced the can with a plastic bottle. "Now spray the leaves."

I pumped the plastic trigger several times for water to rise before it erupted from the nozzle. However, I was spraying just one leaf.

"All of them."

I moved my hand around the plant to wet all the leaves.

When I was done, she said, "Very good. " She placed my creation in my lap, and I looked down in confusion.

"We'll take it to your room," she explained as she unlocked my wheelchair and wheeled it towards the door.

Soon, I was back in my room with a plant on the window sill.

Daily regimen/Christy

As my stay in the hospital progressed, I was getting used to the rhythms of daily routines: get up, shower, have breakfast, and wait for the nurse to wheel me out. I had now settled into a daily physical, occupational, and speech therapy regimen.

I must confess that I had no clue what a therapist did before I had my stroke. To an average person, every activity looks easy. However, for me, each of them was challenging. During the day, nurses came by several times, and doctors made their rounds. By now, I was familiar with most nurses, doctors, and therapists. However, every once in a while, I'd see a new face. I'd make it a point to read and memorize their name tags to associate them with their faces. It was a little mental game I played to keep my memory sharp. Since I was not in a position to read books, I'd read signs—large and small—to exercise my optic muscles.

Once, during a therapy session, the therapist wanted to test my vision. He placed an eye chart a few feet away and asked me to read from top to bottom. I could read not only the letters but also the name of the chart manufacturer.

"You see 20/20," he declared.

I smiled. "More like 10/20." We had a good laugh.

I'm narrating this incident because small events—like these—helped to boost my low spirits.

I was also surprised to see strangers visit me. I say, surprised, because I was not expecting them.

For example, one day, when I lay in my bed, a lady wheeling a small suitcase walked in. She looked very professional in her charcoal-gray business suit. I thought she was lost and had entered the wrong room.

"Yes?" I asked.

"Hi," she said, smiling as she scanned my face. "Do you need a haircut?"

This threw me off. I had not even considered it. Yes, my hair was growing, but it didn't require a haircut—at least not yet.

Do I?

Subconsciously, I raked my fingers through my hair. I wondered how I appeared to other people. As part of my morning routine of getting ready, my wife would put gel on my hair and comb it daily. And my father shaved me every alternate day. Besides, I was too preoccupied with my illness to think about my vanity. I had other things to worry about. Fortunately, my wife had taken over all the other tasks: paperwork, grocery shopping, dropping off and picking up my daughter, etc. My only priority was to get better.

"No, thank you. Not yet."

"No worries at all," she said pleasantly. "If you need one anytime, just inform the nurses."

"Will do."

"Thank you." She turned around and exited the room.

As she was leaving, I heard a dog panting. Soon, a golden retriever entered my room. I was taken aback. A blue vest draped his lustrous golden fur, and a red leash tethered him. Therapy Dog was embroidered on the vest. A smiling middle-aged lady held the other end. She, too, wore the same colored vest. She had a round face. Big round glasses covered it. She had curly white hair.

"Hi," she said, smiling.

"Hi," I said, looking at the panting dog. He was now resting on his hind legs and giving me his doggy look—his mouth open, his tongue hanging from one side, and his eyes softened.

I looked into his expressive eyes, holding my gaze. I wanted to pat him, so I dangled my left hand. He immediately understood what I was trying to do. With his tail wagging, he approached my hand, sniffed it, and gently slid his head below it. I patted him for a while, scratching his head and ears. With his eyes closed in ecstasy, I could see that he was enjoying it.

After a little while, they left to entertain the next patient. I didn't want them to go; I didn't want to be left alone. I was enjoying the innocent dog's company.

Once, an old lady in her sixties came by. She had a kind smile. She told me she was a church volunteer and was there if I wanted to pray together.

I was so consumed in my woes that I had not even considered it. Besides, I am not a religious person. Moreover, the horrible experience I had gone through left me bitter about the whole concept of religion. I was left with more questions than answers.

Even before my stroke, I'd scoff at foolish rituals and traditions. My scientific mind couldn't wrap its head around the concept of religion. Finally, I have resigned myself by saying that *religion and logic can never live together.*

Also, she was here for a good deed. She didn't have an ulterior motive. It would be unfair to unload my woes on her.

"No, thank you," I merely said to the kind lady. "I want to rest."

"Okay," she said as she left.

During my physical therapy sessions, I was constantly with one therapist and sometimes two (depending on the exercises).

Once, a young therapist came by.

"Hi, I'm Christy," she said cheerfully.

"Hi, Christy," I said. "What are we going to do today, the usual floor exercises?"

"Not really," she replied. "Can you swim?"

Swim?! What is she make me going to do today?

"Yes," I said, nodding to hide my surprise.

"Good," she exclaimed.

"Why?"

"Today, we are going to do aqua-therapy," she declared.

She took me to the hospital pool, asked me to change, changed herself into a bathing suit, and guided me to perform aquatic exercises. Getting in the water physically transformed me. I stopped having the fear of falling. My body was straighter.

She didn't have to do this. But I was touched by her selfless gesture. She now has her own rehabilitation center[1].

This effect has stayed with me even now. I feel more confident in my gait whenever I get into a pool. The buoyancy has a miraculous impact on the body.

> Dear reader, if you know anyone with similar difficulty walking, encourage them to try aqua therapy. By far, it's the best exercise.

Occupational therapy was tedious, frustrating, and boring. It required me to perform mundane and repetitive tasks, such as tying a shirt's buttons, untying them and tying them back, peeling a banana, sowing a plant in a pot, writing a letter, hitting a balloon while in a wheelchair, and so many other seemingly everyday tasks. However, I would break into a sweat while performing them. One of the most frustrating exercises was threading a large plastic needle, tying one end, and passing beads through it to make a garland. Another

---

[1] To find out more, please visit precisionrehabilitation.co

challenging exercise was to place pegs in empty holes in a wooden board. Beads of sweat would form on my forehead and coalesce to run down my nose. I would feel them on my half-jutted tongue as I concentrated on the task.

Speech therapy was most relaxing as I had to do little with my body. Only my mouth worked as I spoke. The therapist took notes as I spoke. The most important thing she taught me was to slow down. I would jumble my words as my brain worked faster than my tongue. She also taught me to modulate my voice. I could not gauge the decibel level because I had difficulty hearing from one ear. Even now, sometimes (thank God it's only sometimes), I tend to speak loudly. Also, since English is not my first—or second—language (Gujarati being my mother tongue and Hindi being the other language I speak fluently), I had to 'Americanize' the pronunciations.

Even when a regular Indian speaks, the accent may sound thick to a non-Indian.

When I returned home, I found an organization called the Speech and Language Development Center (SLDC). I was fortunate to be taught by the founder, Aleen Agrowitz[2]. She immediately realized that English was not my first language and patiently worked with me. She had a support group where people like me met.

During our conversations, she discovered that I was a software consultant before my TBI. She then asked me to develop a software system for her school. She would invite me to attend meetings with normal people. That was her way of improving my speech and boosting my confidence.

She would also invite me and others like me (with disabilities) to her house to get to know one another.

---

[2] To find out more, please visit sldc.net/about/

She was a great lady who touched my life.

I have also attended the B.R.A.I.N[3]—Brain Rehabilitation and Injury Network, run by Susan Rueb, where people with similar (or worse) conditions meet.

It is my opinion that in addition to all the therapies, these kinds of support groups help tremendously.

Sheryl Flynn, a Ph.D. physical therapist, also took my case to improve my gait. I used to go to Cal State Long Beach, where she (along with several PT—Physical Therapy—students) would work with me. She founded Blue Marble Health[4], remotely monitoring those with chronic disease and aging.

Urologist

In the early days of my return from USC to Long Beach Memorial, many doctors visited me. As they had already seen me, I was familiar with them. However, I was surprised when I read the specialty embroidered on one doctor's coat. He was a urologist. More than surprised, I was curious about his visit. Why would a urologist visit a stroke patient? There was nothing wrong with my kidneys.

He was a well-dressed young man with a muscular body. His muscles bulged from his expensive, pin-striped blue suit. He had a chiseled face with perfect teeth. He had gelled his neatly combed hair. He wore shiny, wing-tipped brown shoes. He looked more like a model than a doctor. Although he wore a white coat over his suit, he smelled of success. There was a faint whiff of deodorant when he came close to me to check me.

He pressed on the hospital gown where my stomach would be.

---

[3] To find out more, please visit thebrainsite.org
[4] To find out more, please visit bluemarblehealthco.com

I continued to lie inert.

"Hmm," he said. "Can you turn over?"

I looked at the other doctors to come to my rescue.

"Not yet, he can't," one of them said.

"No worries." He reached under my lower back to feel my kidneys.

"How old are you?" he asked me while kneading my muscles.

"Thirty-six." Hearing my age aloud made me realize how young I was. Probably the youngest person in the room.

"Good," he finally exclaimed.

"What?"

"You won't be required to wear a catheter constantly. You are young, and your kidneys are strong."

"Oh, good." I was relieved, not realizing how painful it could be each time I wanted to relieve myself.

While in the hospital, I witnessed several patients having a catheter, with a thin plastic tube disappearing up their gown and the other side ending in a plastic bag to collect the liquid. Being admitted to a hospital itself can be a horrific experience.

We are all used to seeing patients walk the hospital corridors wheeling portable rods with IVs attached to them. In fact, I've witnessed a few such patients smoking when I was wheeled outside the building. I couldn't help but shake my head to see such irony on such occasions. While one tube pumps life into them, the other shortens it.

However, we rarely see patients with catheters. To further add to one's woes, this can be traumatic on many levels. Not only is it painful, but embarrassing. I thank my stars for not being made to go through that.

> Dear reader, if you know anything about how it works, you know how painful the whole process

can be.

A hospital is not a happy place. We would consider ourselves lucky if we didn't have to use it. The maternity ward is the only place of joy I've found in a hospital. A hospital is where one life begins, and the other can end—a true sanctuary for the circle of life.

It truly is a place where life and death live next to each other. In one room, you hear a scream of joy and, in the next, a cry of agony.

Enough of my philosophy. Let's get back to my experience.

Instead of tethering me with a catheter, he gave me medication to stop my urination as I was in no condition to go to the bathroom. It wasn't a great feeling, but I consoled myself by thinking I would not have a tube coming out of me with my urine ending up in a transparent pouch.

The medication had its desired effect. Not only did it stop my urine, but I had no urge to go. They had to scan my kidneys to see if they were full. They had a device similar to the ultrasound machine (probably the same) for that. They would apply cold gel to my stomach and scan me. If the monitor displayed that my kidneys were full, they 'voided' me—a very technical medical term used for relieving. I say void in jest, but it was a serious matter.

I won't describe the gory details of how it's done, but suffice it to say that it involved a thin plastic tube and a lot of pain.

To my relief, they didn't have to void me frequently since I was young. Even the few times were traumatic enough. The doctors told me that I was fortunate that this happened to me when I was young. *Fortunate?!* What the bloody hell? Were they kidding? It shouldn't have happened at all.

The urologist looked at me. From my expression, he must have realized what I was thinking. His voice softened.

"Mr. Aithal, it should not have happened at all," he said with a grave look. "I can't even begin to imagine how hard it must be for you."

I looked at him glumly. *You got that right. You can't even begin to imagine what it feels like. Is this one of your canned sentences? Do you know that doctors can be the worst patients?* I restrained myself from saying it aloud. I was angry then, but now I realize they were all there to help me. They were trying their best to make decisions that would benefit me.

> By the way, anger, erratic behavior, mood swings, etc., are the after-effects of a TBI. The doctors had informed my wife to be prepared for such outbursts and be patient yet firm. A TBI is not only taxing for the patient, but the caregiver also (maybe more taxing).

I looked around the room. "It's okay," I simply said. "I appreciate all your efforts. Without your timely help and guidance, I doubt if I would have survived."

They all acknowledged with a smile or a nod.

The urologist paused for a while. "However," he continued, "If there is any age that this tragedy should befall anyone, the thirties is the right age."

The others nodded in approval.

I didn't want to hear his explanation. *No age is right to fall sick*; I wanted to scream.

"Why?" I asked although I knew what he was going to say.

"Because you are still young and strong. Your body can withstand more blows than if it had to go through the same if you were much older. Your chances of recovery are much greater now. The first year after any brain injury is crucial. The brain is a fantastic organ. It relearns. It will build new neural paths to issue commands. The harder you'll work for the next year, the faster you'll recover."

This piece of advice was given to me by many: doctors, therapists, etc.

Then, what he said has always irritated me whenever I am asked this.

"From one to ten, what's your pain level?"

What's your pain level?

Over the years, I have lost count of the number of times I've been asked what my pain level was. It depends on various factors, such as whether I am walking, standing, or seated. It's tough for me to convey that in a number, but I guess it's a number for a physical therapist to gauge how much they should push me to do exercises.

Even now, when I go for a doctor's visit, I rest in the chair for a few minutes before taking my blood pressure. The very act of walking and climbing a flight of stairs can be taxing on my body.

> Dear reader, listen to your body. It talks to you a lot. *Use it…, but don't abuse it.*

As they say, there are five stages of grief: denial, anger, bargaining, depression, and acceptance. During my hospital stay, I must have oscillated from the first two in the beginning. I was unaware of my feelings. I had more urgent things on my mind. Now I realize I've jumped two stages to find myself in the last stage: acceptance. Once I reached this stage, I found myself comfortable with my condition.

Once again, I must say how fortunate I am to get timely emergency care. This country's infrastructure is very powerful. Not only did the best healthcare and timely assistance in an emergency save my life, but the facilities available to me, such as a gymnasium, a swimming pool, and excellent therapy centers, have let me lead an enriched life after my hospital stay.

I've heard many horror stories: I lost my relative because the ambulance was not able to reach the hospital due to the traffic, once my husband was discharged from the hospital, his condition deteriorated because the facilities for the aftercare were pathetic or non-existent, etc.

People here respect my personal space. They see I'm a little slow in walking and give me space. I am hyper-aware of my surroundings, knowing how a tiny mistake can be costly.

I am able to lead a respectable life here. Whenever I go out, I never worry about finding a parking spot. Even while driving (yes, I drive now), it's a pleasure to do so as everyone (almost everyone) follows the law.

Things just work smoothly here.

Chapter 3

Wanting to go home/smoking

DURING MY FIFTY-THREE DAYS in the hospital, I was wheelchair-bound. My top concern was standing up alone—without any support and walking.

Whenever I was with a therapist, I would ask, "Will I be able to walk?"

At first, they would pretend that they had not heard me. When I'd repeat my question—a bit louder this time, they would always avoid my gaze and say, *"We'll see."*

In fact, towards the end of my prolonged stay, I saw a look of resignation on their faces. They had modified their exercises to a practice routine so I could perform daily activities from a wheelchair, which was very disheartening to my spirits.

In addition, they would train me on how to safely shift from my wheelchair to a regular chair, a sofa, a bed, etc.

They would also place a walker in front of my wheelchair so I could lift myself while I held it. However, I was unable to lift myself without falling, so they went to plan B, the *'wheelchair only'* plan.

However, I was determined to get out of being a wheelchair-bound person for the rest of my life. I was too young. I had many years ahead. I wanted to be as normal as possible.

On the last day of my extended stay, Charlie, my physical therapist, entered my room.

"Hi," he said, smiling.

I beamed.

"Ready to go home?"

"You bet," I said, nodding enthusiastically.

"Great," he exclaimed. "So, today will be your last session. Let's get started."

"Right."

He wheeled me out of my room and headed to the therapy area. When we reached the room, he wheeled me next to the blue bed so I could practice shifting myself out of my wheelchair.

"No."

He raised his eyebrows. "No?"

"Can we practice me getting up?"

"What?" He looked surprised. "You know we can't do that, right? It's too dangerous. You are not ready for it. You can get injured. Besides, you won't have a trained professional when you go home."

"I'm well aware of it. But I insist. Can you place the walker in front of me?" I said with a determined look.

He still looked unconvinced. "Are you sure?" he asked me with a doubtful look.

"Yes," I said, nodding enthusiastically, hoping to convey confidence. However, I was nervous. Butterflies were fluttering in my belly.

"O—okay." He still wasn't convinced. "Hold on. Let me get someone to help."

Is he doing this to emphasize his point that it can't be done by a single person? My wife was young and strong, but I started to doubt that she alone would be able to do it. Besides, she was trained to shift me from a wheelchair. Lifting me from the floor would be a whole new thing.

"Sit tight," he said.

As if I'd get up and go somewhere.

"I'll be right back."

He called for another therapist to assist him. He then went to the corner of the room to grab a walker, flung it over his shoulders, unfolded it when he was near me, and placed it in front of my wheelchair. He then held the gait belt, which was tied around my waist, tightly with both hands. The other therapist was behind me, holding my wheelchair. While he held the wheelchair with one hand, he placed his other hand on my shoulders. They looked at each other and nodded.

"Ready?" Charlie asked.

I nodded.

"If you ever feel woozy, remember, the chair is right behind you."

I nodded again, took a deep breath, grabbed the walker, and willed myself up. My knees were shaky, and I was shaking unsteadily, but I was able to hold on to the walker and stand straight. I grabbed its sides tightly as if I were holding on to life. My heart was pounding. My breathing had quickened. Beads of sweat had formed on my forehead.

A look of astonishment crossed Charlie's face. His jaw had dropped.

He looked at the therapist behind me. "He can stand up." His voice was a mixture of surprise and happiness.

He looked at me. "You can stand up," he said with pride.

I stood for a few seconds—what seemed to be an eternity, wobbly, shaking unsteadily, but proud of my achievement. I then collapsed back into the wheelchair with a thud. I was drained of energy and sweating profusely now. However, I was elated. A silly smile spread across my face with a sense of achievement.

Looking back, I realize that it was the same for Charlie, too. He had worked very hard and diligently on me, and seeing my condition improve must have been a great source of pride for him.

They probably don't realize it, but some souls—like Charlie and Christy—have had a lasting effect on me.

> But, dear reader, I'm jumping way ahead of my hospital saga. Let me take you back several days when I had spent only a few days at the hospital.

As my health improved and I started getting used to the rhythms of the hospital, being visited by nurses, doctors, therapists, etc., I began to get restless. I was homesick.

Whenever a doctor entered my room, I'd first ask him when I'd be released.

"How are you feeling today?"

"Fine. When can I go home?" I'd ask eagerly.

"Not yet, but very soon," he'd reply.

"Do you have a discharge date?"

"No."

"So you don't know when I can go home."

"Very soon," he would repeat.

The full extent of how sick I was hadn't dawned on me yet.

I was silent. I felt like a dark cloud of hopelessness had suddenly entered the room. The doctor looked at my gloomy face. He must have sensed my low spirits. After all—and I'm a firm believer—mental recovery is as vital as physical recovery.

"You need a change," he finally declared, offering a potential solution to my restlessness.

He turned to my wife. "Have you tried sun therapy?"

My wife shook her head.

"Take him outside. The sun will do him good. When he sees others, it'll lift his spirits."

"That's a good idea. His parents will be coming to see him soon. I'll ask them to take him outside."

Soon, my parents arrived. They wheeled me and placed my wheelchair beside a bench where they sat. Although it was morning, I felt the heat on my face. I squinted to shield my eyes from the beating sun. Just then, a nurse walked past us and sat on an empty bench beside us. She was holding a coffee cup. She placed it next to her and fumbled in her pocket. She produced a packet of cigarettes and tapped the box to loosen one out. She held it between her lips and fumbled again for a lighter. She took it out of her pocket, flicked it on, cupped her hand, and brought the dancing flame to the end of her cigarette. Her cheeks concave as she inhaled, and the tobacco that was brown a few seconds ago glowed red. She took a deep drag and exhaled with a smoker's pleasure (it must have been her first cigarette of the day.) A white cloud escaped one side of her lips and wafted towards me. My nostrils flared as I inhaled deep. I closed my eyes in the pleasure of being a second-hand smoker. I realized that I had not smoked since my TBI. Suddenly, my body began to crave for a fix.

Smoking is not just a mental need but a physical need, too. Having been a non-smoker now, I can say that I have tried to quit smoking several times but had failed miserably every time. I've given promises to my wife and daughter every time, only to break them in a few days.

Moreover, it is not only an expensive habit but also very harmful. I admire the folks who have gone cold turkey or have been able to kick this nasty habit while their faculties were intact. Sadly, I had to endure a severe stroke for me to be able to give it up. Even then, in the beginning, my brain played tricks. I began to have an inner dialog about smoking being harmless. To add to this, I had been reassured by the doctors that smoking didn't cause my stroke. However, they had advised me to quit smoking. I probably would have dismissed their advice had I not stayed smoke-free for the fifty-three days in the hospital. I started to breathe better, snore less, enjoy the aroma of various cuisines, and so many such things have benefitted my life.

Also, I didn't realize how I smelled with my smoke-filled clothes. I was desensitized to the foul smell, but people around me had to endure it. Now, my nose is sensitive to the smell of smoke.

Although there is a designated smoking area outside each building, the smoke wafts through, and the non-smokers have to be secondhand smokers, whether they like it or not.

Weighing

One evening, I lay in bed staring at the plant I had potted earlier, wondering who watered it. It was doing remarkably well. Tiny, green leaves were shooting out and leaning towards the window, thirsting for sunlight. The day had ended, and the therapy sessions were over. With nothing to do, I always used to find the evening period between five and eight boring. Eight was when my wife arrived after attending to our children and my family's needs. Many times, I've wondered how she managed to do it. She then would stay with me until the end of the day.

An Asian nurse walked in when I was lying on the bed in my room. She was short and thin in stature and had a pleasant face. She wore a nurse's uniform of light blue trousers and a floral shirt. She also wore white sneakers that squeaked against the sterile and shiny floors. I had seen the nurses wear a similar uniform. They were probably given the latitude of the top—with pre-approved patterns—but always light blue trousers and sparkling white sneakers.

> Dear reader, have you noticed that they are easily identifiable outside their workplace as they usually don't change into civilian attire? However, a doctor is not, as he is always in civilian clothes. All he has to do is put on a white coat and hang a stethoscope around his neck when (s)he is in the hospital, and a physical therapist has to sling a gait belt over one shoulder.

The nurse stood at my bedside. "Hello," she said cheerfully, "I'm Cee."

"Hi, She," I repeated her name but struggled to say it clearly. My tongue felt thick and heavy in my mouth, and I could hear myself mispronouncing her name.

"No, Cee," a bit louder.

"S-she," I repeated, but my tongue wasn't cooperating. Although my brain wanted to say one thing, an entirely different sound would come out of my mouth. The most frustrating part was I could hear myself mispronouncing a word, but the connection between my brain and the tongue had broken. It wanted to do its own thing. It had gone rogue.

I took a deep breath to calm myself down. *Slowly*, my brain commanded, *Cee.*

I'd read that the process of speaking involves several complex steps that affect different areas of the brain and various parts of the body, such as conceptualization, language processing, word retrieval, motor planning, signal transmission, articulation, feedback and adjustment, and so on. However, it was all theoretical knowledge now. All that didn't matter right now. I just wanted to pronounce her name without any effort. When put into practice, if my brain would think about all that was involved in uttering a single word, it would never be able to function normally. It had to come naturally, without any thoughts of theoretical knowledge. It had to be a muscle memory.

"S—s—sh—shhee." *Damn, damn, damn. Wrong again.* It was a straightforward name to pronounce. It merely required the muscles of the mouth. It was not a word that needed the throat or the diaphragm.

I've noticed this phenomenon several times, especially when I try to talk fast. However, I've discovered that I can communicate better if I speak slowly and deliberately (not in slow motion). The opposite person can understand what I want to convey.

However, I still am unable to control the volume of my voice correctly. On several occasions, my wife, daughter, or son has to shush me. I'm sure I do it in front of others, too, but out of courtesy, they tend to ignore this flaw.

"C-e-e," she repeated, slower this time, pointing to the name tag on her shirt with one hand while raising the other to make a fist. She unfolded her thumb, index, and middle finger, each time speaking aloud a single alphabet. "C.e.e, Cee."

"Shh.ee.e, S-s-sh-she," I fruitlessly struggled again. I was not getting anywhere, and my frustration was rising.

She realized I was struggling with my words and smiled patiently. "Never mind. Let's weigh you."

I motioned to get up from my bed so she could transfer me to the wheelchair.

"No, no." She gently pushed down my shoulders. "You stay where you are. I'll be right back."

She then unlocked and wheeled the empty wheelchair out of the room.

What is she doing? I was puzzled. *Doesn't she want to weigh me? Where is she taking the wheelchair without me in it?*

I lay on my bed, waiting for her.

After a few minutes, she reappeared with the wheelchair. "Okay," she declared. "Let's get you in." She helped me transfer to the wheelchair.

By now, I had become an expert in using a wheelchair: raise your feet to allow the person assisting you to lower the footrests, flip them to unfold the footplates, and unlock the wheels.

"Ready?"

I nodded.

"Here we go."

She wheeled me out of the room. She slowed down as we passed the door to navigate cautiously through it.

"Mind your legs." She then increased the speed and went to the end of the wide corridor, past patient rooms. Many of them lay in bed with various monitors attached to them, some with IVs, and some sitting upright with their loved ones around them. Most were above fifty, but some were in their youth.

A nurse passed us with a pile of trays laden with meals for the patients. When she saw Cee, she nodded.

"Hi, Cee."

"Hi, Vera," Cee acknowledged.

See, just Cee. So easy, I thought.

"Where are you headed?"

"I'm on meal-duty, you?"

"I'm going to weigh him."

"Ah."

"Keep a tray for me," Cee joked.

Vera laughed. "Yeah, right. You very well know I can't do that. These are for the patients."

She laughed back. "I know. I'm only kidding."

I envied such casual conversations. They sounded so natural and easy. They flowed between two humans without much thought or effort. They could effortlessly do it while continuing to do their other tasks. They didn't have to stop doing what they were doing in order to converse. I longed for such casual banter.

She wheeled me past the patient rooms.

Where is she taking me? I wondered. My curiosity was momentarily answered.

A closed door stood at the end of the corridor, unlike the patient-room doors, which were wide open. Cee navigated to the door and stopped. She swiped her key card to unlock it (another fixture not found in a patient room) and guided the wheelchair. The motion sensor lights turned on.

We entered a vast room. A large, strange-looking iron contraption lay in one corner. A steel ramp jutted out of its side. She guided the wheelchair up the inclination to a broad platform, locking the wheels securely. She then walked down the ramp and pressed a button on its side. A motorized hum slowly lifted the ramp. She shoved her hand in her pocket to produce a pad and a pencil. She jotted down the numbers flashing on the panel beside the button.

"Okey-dokey," she said cheerfully as she shoved the pad and pencil back. "Done." She pressed the button again to lower the ramp, walked up, unlocked the wheels, and headed back.

I was curious. "What was that?"

"A weighting scale." She stated the obvious. *I know that much*, I thought.

"How does it work? Why did you take an empty wheelchair first?"

"To weigh it first without you and then with you in it."

Duh, of course, I thought. *And you did your B.Sc. in Physics. Shame on you.*

"Have I put on weight?"

"A little," she replied. She was being nice.

I realized why. When I was initially admitted to the hospital, since I couldn't taste anything, I didn't enjoy eating. Thus, I started eating less, which resulted in me losing weight rapidly. However, when the sense of taste returned, it was first sweets. Hence, I probably devoured many sweet things over the period.

Moreover, my family didn't refuse me when I demanded sweets. They were just happy to see that my sense of taste had slowly returned. I had to be careful. Lack of mobility also contributed to my weight gain.

Also, I noticed that the exercises the therapists made me do took a little extra effort. I also noticed that it was a little harder to lift myself from a lying position. Whenever I was shifted into a wheelchair, I would sit with a thud.

Restraint and self-discipline were required. Besides, it was for my good.

Over the years, I've found that I feel much better when I'm lighter. My gait improves, and I'm able to perform more vigorous tasks. When I go to the gym, I can do more reps for longer periods, handle more weights, etc. Losing weight has had enormous benefits.

For me, losing weight is not about looking good. It's no longer about superficial vanity. I want to do it for a more enriched life.

Day pass

As the days progressed, I began to grow increasingly restless. All I wanted to do was go home. Never did I realize the importance of home. We all crave a place that we call home, to be among loved ones, to be in our comfort zone, to do nothing in particular, and to know that people around us want to be with us. I wanted to be among my loved ones in a place of comfort and familiarity.

The burning desire to go home reminded me of the famous dialogue of the hit movie E.T.: *E.T. Go Home.* I then understood the difference between a house and a home—a house is an investment of money, whereas a home is an investment of love. As the saying goes, *home is where your heart is.*

The doctors, nursing staff, and therapists who worked with me sensed my low spirits. During my therapy sessions, I began to do my exercises more mechanically instead of putting my heart behind the effort. They would notice me responding to their talks with a monosyllable answer. A gloomy face now replaced my usual enthusiastic smile. They saw this shift in my mood.

A quick meeting was arranged between the doctors and therapists to discuss a plan of action to boost my low spirits. After all, my mental well-being was as important as my physical state.

I wasn't present at the meeting. Hence, I can only assume what must have transpired.

"What is Mr. Aithal's progress?" asks a doctor.

"Well," replies a therapist, "not good. It has plateaued."

"What do you mean?"

"He was very enthusiastic earlier, but, as the days have progressed, there's a noticeable decline in his progress. He keeps asking when he can go home."

"He has asked us too."

> Dear reader, I believe a hospital is a great place for physical care. However, it is not as great for a person's psyche. Once your loved ones have gone home and you are all alone, trapped in your thoughts, it can be a very depressing place.

One of the therapists said: "I can vouch from past experiences that it'll make a tremendous difference. His is not the first case I've come across. Every patient who had a long stay has always asked the same question. We've seen a dramatic improvement after they have returned as if they have recharged their batteries. They perform all the exercises with more vigor."

Finally, everyone agreed that I needed a change in environment to boost my low spirits.

The day began as any other day. A young doctor entered my room. I had never seen him before. I heaved myself up, readying myself for one more day of therapy.

He greeted me with a wide smile. "Good morning."

"Morning," I mumbled glumly, unable to return his enthusiasm.

"Guess what."

"What?"

"You are going home today."

"Yeah, right," I said. I wasn't amused. It was a cruel joke to play. "Please forgive me if I don't find it funny." I hardened my expression to show him that I was getting angry.

"No, no. I'm serious," he said as he shoved his hand in his coat pocket and produced a paper. "Look."

I looked at it suspiciously.

"What is it?" my eyes narrowed.

"It's a day pass," he replied, waving it in front of my face.

I snatched it from his hand and scanned it. As I read, my eyes changed from a suspicious look to a crinkling smile. I could hardly believe the written words. Fearing the word would magically disappear, I reread the note to ensure my eyes weren't deceiving me.

They had issued me a day pass to visit my home, and I was ecstatic. I looked up at him, smiling ear-to-ear now.

"Thank you." I choked, clutching the paper tightly as if it were a life float thrown to a sinking man. I am not a person who cries easily, but I am sure my eyes must have watered. I felt a sense of exhilaration as if I was being released from captivity. I brought the hand that I was holding the paper into my chest.

"Thank you, once again," I repeated myself, sounding grateful, feeling a little guilty now that I had expressed my anger to him only a little while ago. "I really appreciate it."

"You are welcome," the doctor said kindly. His expression changed to a severe look. "You have to promise to return in the evening," he warned me.

I nodded. "Yes, of course," I said, with a broad smile, hardly being able to conceal my excitement.

By now, the entire nursing staff knew. Every nurse who entered my room had a big smile on their face.

"So, you get to go home," "Don't you like us?" etc., they would kid.

"No way. Sorry, but you are stuck with me for a few more days," I would reply, "I'll be back by the end of the day."

> Dear reader, I can't begin to express my gratitude to them. They have spent the most amount of time on me throughout my stay. According to me, they are under-appreciated. Like any other professionals, some of them just do their job. However, those who go above and beyond their duties have an everlasting impact on a patient's life. Kudos to these great souls.

Soon, my wife arrived. One look at me, and she sensed my high spirits. Something was different. I was bursting to share my joy.

"What?" she asked.

"I'm going home."

"Yeah, right," she said as she, too, had the very same initial reaction.

I handed her the day pass. "Look."

She scanned the note and looked up at me. She was smiling. Her eyes were watering. "I'll be back," she said, wiping her tears.

"Where are you going?"

"To talk with the doctors."

"No," I raised my voice in vehement protest.

"Why?"

My reaction took her aback. She wanted to talk to the doctors, but I didn't want to waste a single minute.

"We have to be back by evening," I said as I swung my legs from the bed. "Move me to the wheelchair."

She then understood my restlessness. She called the nurse for help, who transferred me to the wheelchair and handed it to my wife. She then pushed my wheelchair to the minivan and moved me to the front seat.

"Ready?" she said, turning the keys.

I nodded.

She shifted into the drive and slowly passed the hospital's main gates.

I felt exhilarated as we drove on the surface street. My house is about twenty minutes' drive south of the hospital in the City of Cypress in North Orange County, Southern California. Under normal circumstances, my wife would go south on the 405 freeway to reach there. However, aware of my condition, she drove on the local street as the speed on the 405 would be higher. The doctors had advised her to drive slowly, so my eyes adjusted to the surroundings.

As we moved past grocery stores, restaurants, strip malls, and fast-food places, I admired them as though I were seeing them for the very first time.

Soon, we reached my house. As the minivan turned and parked into the familiar driveway, I could hardly wipe the silly smile off my face. My wife approached my door, transferred me, and wheeled me up the driveway's slope. By now, the therapists had trained her on how to transfer me.

Knees bent. Always tie the gait belt around his waist. Hold him tightly and lift him with your knees still bent; otherwise, you'll strain your back.

It was not possible to enter from the main entrance. My house has a step, and, once I enter, there is a square landing. I had to step down to enter the passageway. We resorted to the only available alternative. She guided my wheelchair to the side yard. We would be entering my house from the back entrance. She turned the wheelchair and backed it slowly, lifting it slightly to clear the small ledge. She then turned me around.

My eyes fell on the smiling faces of my parents. My mother held my son in her arms, and my daughter stood beside her. She immediately ran to me and gave me a tight hug. After a while, she let me go, and my wife guided me to the kitchen table. I noticed they had moved the chair where I usually sat to make room for the wheelchair.

Ours is a two-story house, with all our bedrooms on the second floor. However, when I bought the house, I wanted to have at least one room on the first floor for my aging parents. I didn't want them to climb up the stairs.

Little did I anticipate then that I would be using it one day.

After spending the rest of the afternoon with my family, it was time for me to go back. I didn't want to, but I had little choice. Reluctantly, I said goodbyes. My parents were sad to see me go. My daughter held me tightly and wouldn't let go. My son, although a toddler, sensed that his father was going. He started to wail.

On our way back, we were quiet, mulling in our sorrow. There was nothing remaining to talk about, and both of us knew how the other was feeling.

I had a deja vu. It was a feeling that I had felt once in my past.

I said goodbye to my family and friends at the airport when I left India to come to the US in 1989.

Back in the hospital

Upon my return, I felt like a changed man. My mental batteries were fully charged. Invigorated, I started to go through my exercises with renewed enthusiasm and looked forward to my discharge day.

One day in the late afternoon, I was lying in bed when a middle-aged lady walked in. She wore jeans and a printed cotton shirt, which were a few sizes too loose. Her hair was curly and salt-and-pepper.

"Hello, Mr. Aithal. I'm Carla," she said, pointing to her name tag. "I'm an occupational therapist."

"Hi, Carla," I greeted her. "What are we doing today?"

"Well," she said, smiling. "Something different."

"What do you mean?" My eyes narrowed. *What has she planned for me today?*

"We are going to go out in the community."

"Huh?"

"There's an ice cream shop across the hospital. We'll go there and get some."

I was surprised. "Really?!"

She nodded. "Yes, really."

She then wheeled me out of my room, the hospital, and onto the sidewalk. The vehicles sped past us, and I was terrified. We waited at the signal for the walking light to turn white. After a few seconds, they did, and she wheeled me on the zebra crossing. It was a big intersection. My eyes were on the timer above the signal, counting down until zero. I could feel the tension rising in my head and my pulse quickening. I knew the pedestrians had enough time to walk across, but I was worried as she wheeled me slowly. I sighed in relief only when my wheelchair was safely back on the sidewalk.

She wheeled me across a parking lot to an ice cream shop. The doors swung open as we approached, and a man walked out of the room with an ice cream cone. His eyes fell on us, and he held them wide open.

"Thank you," Carla said.

He smiled. "You are quite welcome," he said, looking at me fleetingly.

We were now in the shop. A few customers were ahead of us. Upon seeing us, they moved aside to make us the first in the queue.

"Thank you," Carla repeated.

We were in front of the counter. Behind it, a young boy wearing a colorful apron with different-sized cones printed across it looked at Carla.

"Yes?"

She pointed at me. "He'll order."

This took me by surprise. I was not ready for it. I was unsure of my communication skills. I gave her a panicked look.

She realized my fear. "Don't worry. I'm here to help you. Go ahead. What flavor do you like?"

"Chocolate."

"Cone or cup?" he asked.

"Cup," I replied.

"Me too," Carla added.

He nodded and loaded two rich brown ice cream scoops in the cup. "Here you go" he said, handing it to us with a flair.

Looking back, I suspect I was not the first person Carla had taken out for ice cream. The whole routine was pre-planned to integrate me into society. It was designed to boost my confidence. It encompassed not just occupational therapy but speech therapy, too. Ice cream shop was just an object. She was working on my confidence to go to any establishment—stores, restaurants, etc.—and converse with people. It worked.

At that time, I was a little apprehensive about it; however, now I see its rewards. That exercise boosted my confidence. I can happily say that I am confident I can converse with strangers.

> Dear reader, Please encourage yourself (or anyone you know who has undergone a similar traumatic injury) to do them diligently—no matter how boring, frustrating, or annoying they may be. They do work!

As days progressed, the doctors started to discuss my discharge date. Also, and I found out later, there was a lifetime limit on the type of insurance I had, and, having been hospitalized for fifty-three days, I would soon hit it. Toward the end of my stay, every day of my stay, therapies, etc., had to be pre-approved by them. I was in no condition to deal with them. My wife handled all that.

The therapists began to train my wife on how to take care of a disabled, fully-grown adult. It's one thing to attend to a toddler and a whole different thing to care for an adult. Minor details—we all take for granted in our daily lives—suddenly became highly important. They would ask all sorts of questions.

Describe your house. How many levels do you have? Do you have any steps to the main door? Do you have a room on the first floor? Is there a full bathroom on the first floor? Is it a walk-in shower or a tub? Do you have any handlebars to grab on? Do you have a maid to help you with your daily chores?

They also considered building a ramp on my front porch and modifying our minivan to fit it with equipment that would suit my needs.

I was always present when this was being discussed between my wife and the therapist, as if I wasn't present. Although everything they talked about was for my safety, I felt helpless. I realized that they were making all these modifications so I could lead an everyday life out in the community; it was a dark time. A feeling of hopelessness had engulfed me.

I started to wonder if this was how I was going to lead the rest of my life. I had so much to look forward to. I had to see my children grow up, attend parties, weddings, and all other functions, travel, and see the world. Hearing this being discussed made me more determined to lead as normal a life as possible. I realized that I had been dealt the worst hand in my life. I had to turn it into a winning hand.

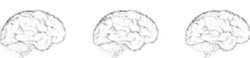

However, there was a problem. As I have narrated earlier, the doctors had given me medication to stop my normal kidney functions. They had to start. I had to relieve myself independently, without any external instruments inserted. Our house was not equipped with an ultrasound machine; besides, there wouldn't be a trained professional around. They would not release me till I could accomplish this task that comes naturally to us.

I was distraught. The logical side of my brain told me it made sense, but the emotional side of it was distressed. No matter how hard I tried to will myself to go, I was unsuccessful for a few days. I would try to breathe down in my stomach, hold it, and push it inward for the kidneys to start working till my face turned red. Only when I could no longer hold my breath would I give up and start breathing normally. I would try it again after a while but was unsuccessful.

"Have you gone?" was the first question the doctors and nurses asked me as soon as they entered my room. When I shook my head, their hopeful expression turned into a concern. In fact, it had now been replaced with customary greetings: *good morning, hi, how are you feeling*, etc. And it wasn't just the doctors, but the nursing staff and the therapists. The nursing staff was more concerned as they would be the ones who would have to void me, and, just like me, they, too, were not looking forward to this unpleasant experience.

"Oh, don't worry," "It'll happen," "Be patient," and so many other platitudes were casually mentioned. However, it's much easier to be a giver than a receiver. I was panicking. The turmoil I felt can't be described.

Finally, on the third day, it happened. It was early in the morning. I had just woken up, so I knew my kidneys would be full. I shut my eyes tight. I breathed in deep and held my breath. I then pushed my stomach to collide with my kidneys. I suddenly felt a rush of relief. I let go of my breath with an ecstatic smile. I was able to relieve on my own accord. A sense of exhilaration mixed with freedom engulfed me.

When the nurse walked in and looked at my smiling face, she didn't ask me the dreaded question. "Yes?"

I smiled. "Yes."

She gave me a thumbs-up. "Alright." She immediately walked out to inform the doctors, who called my wife.

When she arrived, I couldn't stop smiling. She, too, was glad that this phase of my life was over. I would be in a familiar environment. I would see my children, my parents, my friends, and my loved ones.

She had to do some paperwork for my discharge. The doctors and the therapists were giving her instructions on how to attend to me at home.

However, I was getting restless. "Can't you do that over the phone?" I complained.

"Yes, but—." She stopped when she saw my annoyed face. She immediately turned to them, "I'll call you or swing by later. For now, let's finish the paperwork."

I smiled.

I was going home.

Homecoming

On the day of my discharge, there was excitement in the air. My wife had arrived early in the morning. Almost all the nurses who cared for me visited me, and even those not on duty made it a point to come by.

Almost all the therapists, too, came by to give us a few last-minute tips—more like reminders.

"Don't forget to bend your legs." "Lift him from your knees, not your back." "Always use a gait belt." "Don't hesitate to call us for additional tips."

They would then turn to me, "Ready to go home?" "You must be very excited." "Don't forget to do your exercises daily; make it a habit," or such variations of advice were freely given.

"Have the doctors come by today to give you instructions on your medications?" one of them asked.

Thankfully, I was not on any medications. I shook my head. "No. Don't need any."

Eventually, it was time for me to leave the hospital. I had mixed emotions. On one hand, I was sad to leave the place that had saved my life; on the other hand, I was thrilled to leave the place that had kept me for fifty-three days.

After bidding emotional goodbyes to the doctors, the nursing staff, and the therapists, my wife wheeled me outside the hospital. On our way, she laughed. "Did you realize you were thanking those who didn't even attend to you?"

But I didn't care. It was just a blur to me. I just wanted to go home.

As the doors slid open, I squinted as I was wheeled from the temperature-controlled building into bright sunlight.

She navigated me to the curb and locked the wheels. "I'll be right back," she said as she walked to the parking structure.

Momentarily, the familiar white minivan exited, drove towards me, and came to a standstill near me. My wife came around, unlocked my wheelchair, and guided it near the wide-open passenger door. She bent her knees (as taught by the therapists), lifted me while she held the belt on my pants, and gently transferred me.

"Mind your head," she warned me. She then buckled me in, shut the door, and folded my wheelchair to store it in the trunk.

"Ready?" she asked as she turned on the keys.

"Yes," I said. I looked around. I fiddled with a few knobs. I turned around to see my son's car seat. I flipped the visor above me to look at my face in the mirror. The familiarity of the interior warmed my heart.

She shifted the gear to D and drove slowly. I looked at the large building that had housed me with mixed emotions. I heard the siren of an ambulance and shuddered. *One more emergency,* I thought. *No one should ever go through what I've endured.*

Little did I realize then that there was more to come. I had already started planning what I would be doing the day I reached home, the next day, the next week, and so on. However, fate had a different plan for me.

"Do you want some music?" my wife asked, snapping me back from my philosophical thinking.

I nodded, and she turned it on. Soft music started to play around me. I gently began to bob my head with the rhythmic beats, but I noticed I was slightly off. I didn't pay much attention to it then, but I think that was my first encounter with music where I was slightly off. That is not to say I don't enjoy a good song now. However, I feel that there's something different.

Instead of taking a right on the surface street leading to our house, she continued to drive straight.

I looked at her. "Where are we going?"

"On 405," she replied.

I was nervous. I was going on the freeway after a long time. I held tight to the side handle above my window as she turned onto the on-ramp. The meter was on. There was a car ahead of us, waiting for the light to turn green. As soon as it turned green, it sped forward with tires screeching. It was our turn now. The minivan slowly inched forward and came to a halt near the red light. My pulse quickened in anticipation. Both of us were eagerly looking at the light, waiting for it to turn green. Momentarily, it did, and my wife pressed on the gas pedal. With a lurch, the van took off (thankfully, no screeching of tires was involved).

As the minivan merged into the traffic, she increased its speed to go with the flow. I inhaled deeply, gasping for air. My stomach fell. My eyes widened. My head began to throb. My vision blurred. I felt like I was in a speeding plane about to take off from the runway.

"Slow down," I screamed.

"Huh?" my wife looked at me, confused. Then she looked down at the dashboard. "I'm just going at 50. I'm below the speed limit. Are you okay?"

I shook my head in terror. "No."

I was not okay. My pulse had quickened, and I could feel my heart pounding rapidly. My head was spinning. I was unable to focus. The cars in front of me seem to be turning around. I held tightly to the handle above the window until my knuckles whitened.

"Get off the freeway," I yelled.

She looked at me in alarm. "Okay."

I assume she must have thought, *"We left the hospital less than fifteen minutes ago, and I don't want to take him back there.*

She immediately turned her steering wheel to take the next exit.

"We'll drive on the local roads. Relax. Take a deep breath. You are okay."

However, I remained tense until she took the exit. Only then did my pulse slow down. I started to breathe normally.

The minivan came to a halt at a red light. When the lights turned green, it turned left. Our speed was now considerably slower, and I was grateful to all the traffic lights that turned red, further slowing down our speed.

"What's the very first thing you want to do when we reach home?" she asked, looking straight and concentrating on the road.

Her question took me by surprise. I had thought of several things I wanted to do when I went home, but I had not really thought of the very first thing I would do. *Hug my children? Enjoy a home-cooked meal by my mother? Sleep in my own bed? Meet my friends? Go for a long drive with my wife, along PCH? et cetera, et cetera.* I really couldn't decide. When I was in the hospital, I had fantasized about this moment. But now, the moment was here; my mind was overwhelmed by the choices I could make.

Soon, the minivan turned into our track. The familiar lush green lawns of the vast park at the corner of our track made me smile. After several stop signs, we turned right to our corner house. As my wife pressed a button to open the garage door, I was greeted by the smiling faces of my family.

She opened the rear door of the minivan and proceeded to unload the wheelchair.

I shook my head. "No."

Although we had the wheelchair in the car, I didn't need it for short distances as I had graduated to a walker.

"Are you sure?"

"Yes."

She reached for the walker, unfolded it, and placed it before me. Clumsily, I clambered out of my seat, tightly held the walker, and steadied myself. I was sweating. A simple effort was exhausting. I'm sure that if my blood pressure and heartbeats were measured, they would be highly elevated. Very slowly and cautiously, I navigated through the laundry room and the passageway to the combined family room-cum-kitchen, all the while considering myself fortunate that we had carpets instead of tiled floors. If I lost my balance and fell, the carpet would absorb it better than a bare floor.

Sure, it was a minor observation, but it was crucial for me.

In fact, over the years, I've noticed myself being aware of little things that an average person would take for granted. Whenever I go to a restaurant, I'm scoping my surroundings. What is the parking situation? How far is the restaurant's main entrance from the parking lot? Are there any steps in front of the main entrance? Where are the restrooms situated? How close are the adjacent tables? I must say that my family and friends are sensitive to my needs. Not once have they made me feel different.

Special? Yes. Different? No.

My wife had converted the room on the first floor from my son's playroom to my bedroom. I went to the daybed in the corner and lay down.

The familiar surroundings of a home put me at ease. Within minutes of closing my eyes, I fell asleep.

Homeopathy

I'm from India. Growing up there, Homeopathic medicines were a significant part of my life. It is one of the two most popular medical disciplines there, the other being Ayurveda. Modern science in the West follows the allopathic medical field, and it's a wonderful field for a quick recovery. Also, it is the only discipline people use worldwide that involves surgeries, x-rays, MRIs, mending a fracture, and many other illnesses that require urgent attention. However, many prefer Ayurvedic or Homeopathic medication for long-term chronic illness. Many Indian households (including mine) worldwide will carry several Ayurvedic remedies as alternative cures to minor ailments. They see it as a more holistic approach to the human body—with no side effects.

Unlike allopathic medicines, which offer instant relief, homeopathic medicines require time and patience. That is why they are not popular in a society that is used to instant gratification. The same is true for Ayurvedic treatments.

It was tough to find a doctor who dispensed these medicines. Besides, they cannot be prescribed and are not readily available in drug stores as off-the-shelf medicines. Hence, they were dispensed at the doctor's clinic instead of prescribed.

> Dear reader, remember, this was in 2001. Google was in its infancy. It wasn't as easy as googling a 'homeopathic doctor' and finding one nearby in seconds. Besides, the first smartphone was six years away from its introduction. Looking back, I sometimes wonder how I survived without information available 24/7 at my fingertips.

Finally, we found one after a long search of doing it the old way—talking to my doctors, our friends, etc. Someone told us that there was one homeopathic doctor, and he dispensed medicines at his clinic. I was excited, but my excitement was short-lived when I looked him up. His clinic was forty-five miles east of us, over an hour's drive. But I had minimal choice. I was desperate, willing to try anything that worked. Hence, we decided to go to him.

However, there was a problem. I was still in no condition to drive. Besides, I would be breaking the law even if I could, as my license was suspended. Unbeknownst to me, the hospital had informed the Department of Motor Vehicle (DMV). It's a very routine thing to do.

> Dear reader, California is a very vast state with a less-than-desirable public transport system. Being able to drive is a must. Anyone who has been to California can vouch for that. In fact, people from India prefer to visit the East Coast as it's easier to travel by train there.

My wife noticed the hesitation on my face. "What are you thinking?" she asked me.

"Nothing."

"C'mon. Why are you hesitant? This is great news. We have finally found the right doctor."

I nodded. "Yes," I said, "but."

"But what?"

"Er."

My mind was fighting with itself. On the one hand, I was looking forward to seeing the doctor, while on the other, I wanted to be the one behind the wheel. She knew what was going on in my mind.

"Is it because I've got to drive you there?"

I looked at her sheepishly and nodded.

"What kind of chauvinistic nonsense are you talking about? Even if you could drive, I would be accompanying you, right?"

I nodded.

"So, what's the big deal?"

"Well …"

Her following sentence immediately put my concerns to rest.

"I'll drive you there."

"Are you sure?" I asked, knowing that I would usually be the one driving. However, I was relieved that we had come to a solution—yes, a solution. Not being able to drive was a big problem, but looking back, it was only a problem in my mind.

"Of course," she said as she patted me and got up. She walked to the kitchen drawer, opened it, and rummaged through it until she found what she was looking for: a piece of paper with the doctor's details.

"I'll make an appointment," she said as she lifted the receiver from the phone's cradle and began to dial.

"Thank you." I smiled and added, "for everything."

But she didn't hear me as she had already started to talk on the phone.

My wife drove me to the clinic on the day of the appointment. In fact, over the years, she has accompanied me to every doctor's visit, taken me to all my rehabilitation visits, and sat outside while I was working on improving myself.

We took 91 East. The clinic was in Riverside. One of the good things about a long drive was that we could drive in the carpool lane with less traffic since there were two of us. Those who have driven in the notorious L.A. traffic can relate to the pleasure of driving in a carpool lane.

As we neared our destination, the traffic thinned. We were headed east, away from the ocean. The dry heat of the desert replaced the coolness of living near the Pacific.

Thankfully, his clinic was located near the freeway. Once we exited, we reached it after a few minutes. As I entered, I blinked to adjust them to the shaded interiors from the bright sunlight outside. Although we had started early, hoping to be the first ones to see the doctor, we were disappointed to see that there were a few already ahead of us. Also, the doctor had not arrived yet. I, being a stickler for punctuality, was already upset.

"He's not even here," I complained. "This is nonsense. Why are doctors the only ones who make you wait?"

My wife pacified me. "Calm down. They are not the only ones. And besides, it's not like we have a choice."

"Hmpf," I grunted indignantly.

However, what she said made sense. I didn't have a choice.

Eventually—after a long wait—he arrived. There was a murmur spread through the room. Soon, the first patient was called in. My spirits rose in anticipation that it would soon be my turn, but my enthusiasm was short-lived. The doctor took too agonizingly long to see each of us. Unlike a regular doctor's office, where the doctor comes to the patient while he waits in a room, the doctor would call the patient to see him in his office. However, I was used to this setup as I had experienced it when I was in India.

I patiently waited for hours. After making us wait for hours, the doctor finally saw us for a whole five minutes. I was angered and disappointed. Like other patients, I thought he would spend some time examining me. But it was not to be. He merely wrote a bunch of medicines on paper and instructed me to take them to the front desk, where they dispensed the medication. Furthermore, to add to my disappointment, he had just prescribed only one homeopathic medicine. All others were supplements.

"This is not going to work," I complained to my wife on our way back.

However, she convinced me to be patient and give it a few more tries. "Be patient. Give him some time. Let him work on you. You can't just dismiss him in a single visit."

I laughed sarcastically. "Work on me? He hardly spent five minutes with me."

"I know, and I'll tell him about it during our next visit. But, for my sake, try him out for some more time. After that, I won't pressure you to go to him. Promise."

It was impossible to argue with someone willing to drive me for over an hour to make me better. So, I followed her suggestion and went on several long journeys. Needless to say, it didn't work. However, on the bright side, I did what I loved a lot. To go on a long drive, the only downside being that I wasn't driving. As we neared our city, the traffic increased. Soon, we exited, and the minivan headed to our home on the surface street.

Suddenly, my stomach rumbled in hunger. I realized that I had not eaten anything other than a cup of coffee since morning. I started to look forward to a home-cooked lunch.

Finally, what convinced her was the heat therapy. During this therapy, I was made to lie down on a bed while they switched on an infrared lamp and focused its hot beam on me. I lay there—inert—for thirty minutes while the rays did their thing. A technician sat beside my bed, reading a novel. In the end, I was given the bill. My eyes widened. The charges were ridiculously high.

The technician must have noticed my surprise. "Don't worry. You don't have to pay. We'll change it to your insurance company."

What? Do you realize how insurance works?

They just pass the cost back to the consumers. No wonder it is sky-high in this country. I wanted to scream, but I decided to stay silent. After all, it was the insurance that paid my bills when I was in the hospital for fifty-three days. There is no way I could have afforded the expenses.

Chapter 4

Halfway house

IMMEDIATELY AFTER BEING DISCHARGED, I would go to a house geared towards my transition to a regular life. It was run by the hospital, minus the usual objects one would find at a typical hospital. Instead, it was built like a regular house with a family room, kitchen, and a living room overlooking a courtyard—a flight of stairs led to the bedrooms.

Jokingly, I referred to it as a halfway house. But in all seriousness, it helped me tremendously. It had all the therapists: physical, occupational, and speech. However, the setting was a home as opposed to a hospital.

My wife would drop me off in the morning and pick me up by late afternoon. During the day, they would make me perform regular chores around the house: sweep the floor, wash my dishes while standing in front of a sink, and do many more activities.

Other patients like me would come there; however, the difference was that they wore regular clothes rather than hospital gowns. The only telltale sign was the gait belt tied around their waists.

The intention was to make me feel comfortable while transitioning into my regular life. It wasn't enjoyable in the beginning. At home, I would do all these house chores without any thought. Like any other person, I did it as a daily routine. However, when I had to do it as an exercise while being supervised by a therapist, it suddenly became an annoying chore. Also, some physical activities changed daily so they were not monotonous. They would vary from sweeping the floor to dusting the sofa. However, one thing constant was me being tethered by a gait belt and a therapist always behind me. All of us would sit around a large wooden table for lunch. That was our time to socialize. The speech therapist would start the conversation, and we would then join. By the end of our lunch, the table would be a cacophony of boisterous people. We would then go to the sink to wash our dishes while being closely monitored by an occupational therapist. After a short break, our physical therapy sessions began.

For the fifty-three days of my stay at the hospital, I was wheelchair-bound. Only on the very last day, I stood up, and that too with the aid of a walker. Since then, I have relied upon a walker to stand up. I would hold tight on the sidebars and heave myself up from sitting to standing—albeit wobbly, and vice versa.

It was time for me to stop relying on the walker. While I was doing my physical activities, the therapist would casually talk to me to find out about my home routine. It started with innocuous questions.

"Who lives with you?" she asked one day when I was sweeping the floor with a broom. I had just finished my lunch, and, instead of giving me a break, she had taken me out to the courtyard. She stood behind me, holding the gait belt I was tethered with.

"Usually, there are four of us, my two children and my wife, but right now, there are six of us as my parents are visiting me from India."

"Oh, nice. You have a full house, huh?"

"Yes," I replied.

"You missed a corner."

"Huh?"

She pointed to the floor to show me what she meant.

"Oh, right," I said, concentrating on sweeping the corner.

"Very good."

I beamed. We continued in silence for a while. I stopped and looked around the courtyard. It had a concrete ground with a circular fountain in the middle, devoid of any water—bone dry. She slowly nudged me by pulling at the gait belt. I continued sweeping the ground, which was scattered with fallen leaves. We both were silent. The only sound was the swishing of the broom.

"Describe your house," she said, suddenly breaking the silence.

"Huh? Oh, right. It's a two-story single-family home."

"Nice. How many bedrooms does it have?"

"Four."

"Are all of them upstairs?"

I shook my head. "No. One of them is downstairs. It was my son's playroom before my stroke. We have now converted it into my bedroom. But I want to sleep in my own bed."

"You missed that area." She pointed to the ground near the wall as she guided me there.

I continued to sweep in silence.

"Slowly and deliberately. There's no rush. The leaves aren't going anywhere. The idea is to get your muscle memory back. You should be able to do it effortlessly."

Easy for you to say, I thought. I was already sweating profusely. My clothes were soaked, and now they were clinging to my skin.

"Can we go inside?"

"In a bit. How do you move about in your house?"

"With a walker, but I hate it."

"Why?"

"I want to be able to walk on my own, like a healthy person."

"Hmm." She made a mental note. To my relief, she led me inside. She guided me to the sofa. I collapsed on it with a thud.

"That was bad," she admonished me.

"Huh?"

"You should sit down gently."

"Okay," I said, nodding as if I was absorbing her instructions. However, I wasn't listening to her. I had closed my eyes and enjoyed the relief of cool air caressing my face.

I was just grateful that the day's sessions were over and that my wife would soon pick me up.

The following morning, I was sitting on the armchair. The walker was in front of me. The therapist entered the room in her jogging suit. She was a jogger. She had come back from her morning run.

"Good morning," she greeted me absentmindedly, placing two fingers below her neck to feel her pulse and counting them with her wristwatch.

I nodded. "Good morning."

"Give me a few minutes." She looked up. "I'll go change."

"Sure."

Briefly, I felt a pang of envy. The simple act of going for a run had triggered this emotion. When I was in the hospital, I never felt that way as I never saw people outside their professional environment.

After a few minutes, she reappeared in jeans and a tee, with the familiar gait belt flung on her shoulder.

"Ready?" she asked as she approached me and tied the gait belt tighter than usual.

I grunted as I started to reach for my walker to lift myself. But my eyes widened in surprise (more like terror) as she moved it to the side and out of my reach.

"No, no," she said, shaking her head.

What is she doing?

"We won't be needing that today," she declared.

"Why?" I looked at her, trying to hide my fear.

"We'll practice you standing up from a sitting position without the walker."

I looked at her, conveying my feelings with a stern expression. However, she ignored it. "Didn't you say yesterday that you hated it and wanted to walk on your own?"

I grudgingly nodded.

"Well, this is it then. Let's work on it."

She held me tight and assisted me in getting myself from a sitting position.

"Bend forward. Don't use the armrest to lift yourself. Put your hands on your knees. Use your knees to lift your body. Slowly. I'm right here. Look at me. I'm holding you tight. I won't let go. Do you trust me?"

I nodded, took a deep breath, and followed her instructions. While it would be effortless for any other human being, it was a massive task for someone with limited mobility.

"Very good."

However, I wish I was feeling good. Instead, I was terrified. I felt as though I was standing on the ledge of a high-rise. I wobbled unsteadily, and she tightened her grip.

"Steady. Try to stay still for a few seconds before you step forward."

Step forward? Is she crazy? I must have cursed her then, but I am so grateful now. Gingerly, I took a step forward.

"Awesome. You are doing very well. Now, the left leg."

We continued for a few more minutes until I could no longer do it. She guided me to the chair and made me sit down. I plopped myself with a thud.

"That was great, but, once again, your sitting was not gentle. We need to work on that, too."

Ignoring her, I closed my eyes, relieved to rest in the cozy armchair's comfort.

For the first time in my life, I had acrophobia. Of course, since then, I have become comfortable with it, and I no longer have it. The only fear that has stayed with me until now is claustrophobia.

I think it has to do with my experience in the MRI machine. Even now, when I have to get an MRI, I dread it. I have to take a Xanax to relax me.

I went to the halfway house for a short period—maybe a few weeks—but it helped me tremendously. The repetitive tasks may have been tedious, but they helped me a lot in my recovery.

Aqua therapy/writing practice

When I was in the hospital, Dr. Adams was one of the doctors who saw me regularly. After my discharge, he was my rehab doctor, whom I continued to visit periodically. He would closely monitor my progress and guide me on my path of recovery.

He recommended Dr. Ikeda for my vision therapy. Yes, vision therapy, as he not only checked my vision but also made me perform several exercises to improve it, improving my balance.

He would make me walk on a wooden beam—like a gymnast—only it would be placed on the ground rather than a few feet high. Although my vision had improved a lot, I still had double vision. I would do several exercises to strengthen my eye muscles to remedy that. Gradually, my vision began to improve.

During one of my visits with Dr. Adams, he recommended aqua therapy. "Have you tried it?"

I had never heard of it before.

"What is it? What does it entail?" I asked curiously.

"It's a therapy in water. Do you have a swimming pool at home?"

"No," I said, shaking my head.

"Let me see if there is a pool near your house," he said as he reached for a folder. "Where do you live, in which city?"

"Cypress."

"Hmm," he said as he leafed through the folder.

"Ah," he exclaimed as he found the one he sought.

He took out the leaflet and handed it to me.

I looked at him. "Cal State Long Beach?"

"Yes," he said, nodding. "That's your best option. It's closest to your house."

However, I was unsure.

"There's a number on it. Call them."

"Okay," I agreed reluctantly. "You think it'll help me?"

"Well," he replied, "it can get quite overwhelming if you introduce many gadgets. Just start with walking in water. It'll make a lot of difference."

"How?"

"In many ways. You will improve your gait. Your balance will get better rapidly as you won't have the fear of falling to the ground. You will feel much lighter. And as you know, you will weigh less in water, thus increasing your buoyancy."

Of course.

Upon returning, I called the number. After a few rings, a man answered.

"Hello, is it Cal State Long Beach?"

"Yes."

"Am I talking to the pool department?"

The man laughed. "There's no such thing as a pool department, but, yes, I'm the pool supervisor."

"Great."

"How can I help you?"

I hesitated. "Er."

"What do you need?"

"I was wondering if your pool was open to the public?"

"No."

"Oh," I sighed.

He sensed the disappointment in my voice.

"Why?"

I spent the next five minutes explaining my situation.

"Hmm," he said as he understood my particular need. "And you're not a student here, right?"

"No."

The line was silent for a minute.

"Please," I begged.

I could feel him looking for a way to help me.

"Tell you what?" he finally said.

"What?"

"You can make use of the pool."

"Oh, thank you."

"But, there is one thing."

I was willing to do anything. "What is it?"

"The water polo team comes to practice in the morning. Make sure you come early. They arrive at eight o'clock, so you must leave before that." He repeated the time to ensure its importance. "Before eight o'clock."

"Sure."

I thanked him again. He was doing me a favor.

Fortunately, the pool was very close to where we lived. We would reach the facility at seven and leave by a quarter to eight. My wife and I were the only two souls in the giant Olympic-sized swimming pool. Steam danced on its surface —calm, undisturbed water due to the temperature difference between a heated pool and the outside air. The pool was eerily silent when there was no noise of splashing.

Not only did my wife drive me there, but she also joined me in the pool to hold my hands while I practiced walking. Dr. Adams was right. Being waist-deep in the water did wonders for my posture. I noticed myself standing more erect. Also, I looked straight ahead instead of constantly looking down at the ground, as I no longer feared falling. Not only was I happy, but also more confident. Also, the mere ability to stand straight and converse with someone instead of looking up from a wheelchair does wonders for a person's self-esteem. It's merely a difference of a few feet in height but a difference of day and night.

Having been in a wheelchair before, when I see someone in one, I know how it feels.

When I was not in the pool, the therapists constantly corrected my posture: "Look forward, don't look down, there's nothing in front of you but the ground," "Stand straight," etc. It's easier said than done. However, I could see the difference the moment I got out of the pool. I could feel my body tilting slightly forward. My gaze switched to the ground before me instead of looking forward.

Moreover, my senses were hyper-aware because I was now on a wet and slippery surface. I would dig my toes in to get a better grip. I would walk gingerly, and my steps would be considerably shorter. However, it was worth it.

The other exercise to improve my coordination (yes, there are many) is to practice writing. Writing is a lost art in this era of communicating via a keyboard. The current generation seems to have its own shorthand language filled with emojis. On several occasions, I've tried to decipher what they are trying to say but have failed miserably. Sometimes, I wonder if they realize how life was before smartphones.

Holding a pen between your fingers, the sound of the nib scratching the paper—to give your brain feedback that the nib has hit the surface and not to press your hand any farther—works wonders for the dexterity of holding delicate objects. In this modern era of computers, writing has become an art form. People tend to use a keyboard with thousands of fonts instead of personalizing their style. Some also prefer cursive fonts to email a letter.

> Dear reader, when was the last time you wrote a letter? Signing a check or jotting down a phone number doesn't count. When did you actually pen down a five-hundred-word letter (not email or text a sentence or two or, even worse, use an emoji—the ultimate shortcut to convey one's feelings)? There is no replacement for the art of actual writing.

> As a software developer who loves computers, I, too, confess to preferring typing on a keyboard. It's cleaner and consistent, but it lacks that personal touch.

To me, it was an exercise. Repetition of strokes and curves and being able to take dictations not only helped me improve my handwriting but also made my brain fire the proper commands. The idea was to do it slowly and intentionally until it kicked in as something (someone without my condition) as a natural task. *Write between the two lines. If it's a d, ensure the line extends above the guides. If it's a g or p, extend it below.*

I would then practice my signature. It's way different than actual writing: the curves, the flair, the line below my name with two dots. My hand had to move quickly enough to do it in one go, without lifting the nib, and in cursive. It sure was challenging in the beginning. I lost count of how many times I signed my name. Moreover, my signature needed to match the old one I signed on all the legal documents.

It was more challenging when I dealt with financial institutions in India. They had my old signature on record. Whenever I had to deal with them, which involved my signature, the document would be returned to me due to the signature not being the same. I then would have to fill in several forms, affix my recent photograph with my current signature across it, mail it to them, cross my fingers, and hope that the documents would be accepted. The whole process would take over a month.

Practicing writing was a tedious exercise but worth it.

I have never been an artist, so I didn't expect to draw a masterpiece. I merely wanted to get back to my normal state. It was a dull task (just like many other boring and monotonous tasks), but all these small, mundane, and repetitive tasks helped me improve overall.

One thing I've learned over the past years is to be patient. Time heals a tragedy.

The other exercise my speech therapist made me do was read aloud. It didn't matter what I read: a book, letter, newspaper article, or magazine article. The idea was not only to improve my speech but also to put emotions into the sentences I was reading.

Hearing my voice helped me on two levels. It flexed my vocal cords and controlled my volume.

The Pyramid

I also went to The Pyramid at Cal State Long Beach as part of my daily regimen. It's called that due to its pyramid shape. It's a massive, black structure that houses a multi-purpose arena. At its bottom, it houses basketball courts; above it, there is a student gym. A lush green baseball field was situated on one side of The Pyramid. Behind it was a football field, and in front was the parking lot.

In the corner of the gym is a room for people with special needs to exercise.

Also, it allows the students to see real-life examples of people with various disabilities. It may be embarrassing to the patient; they may feel like (s)he is a circus act in the middle of an arena with hundreds of eyes watching them. However, seeing someone who has already gone through it is a great learning exercise for future therapists. Exercise also varied from physical therapies to occupational therapy. However, they never involved speech therapy. By now, my speech had returned. However, it was a lot slower and slurred. I was aware of my speech impediment, especially when I would tend to talk rapidly. But I was glad that I could communicate.

Even now, after so many years, I tend to jumble up my speech when I try to talk rapidly. I then remind myself to slow down.

Over time, my wife had learned to optimize her time. She would drive me there and drop me off to do my exercise while she went grocery shopping.

After all, she had to attend to the needs of the rest of my family. My children were too young to drive, and my parents, who came from India, didn't drive. So, she was the only driver in our family.

Apart from her duties as a wife, a mother, and a daughter-in-law, she also had the added burden of doing paperwork and making sure all the bills were paid. Usually, our responsibilities were divided. I took care of all the paperwork while she ran the household. However, her responsibilities had doubled. In addition to her regular duties, she now had to take care of everything I did. As they say, it takes two to tango. She now had to dance on her own, without a partner.

At the pyramid, the gym was always teeming with students. It looked even more crowded because all the equipment was placed very close to each other. It was a very narrow place to walk. I remember this vividly. As part of my therapy, I was made to navigate through the students and equipment while being tethered by the gait belt. That was my reintroduction to a crowded place.

My social life, too, had curtailed a lot. I now preferred going to a get-together with fewer people, and that too with those who knew my condition.

That is because of self-preservation. If a stranger had to see me, looking at my outward appearance, he would assume nothing was wrong with me. I would not have a typical identifying object: a wheelchair, walker, walking stick, etc. My desire to be as normal as possible was like a double-edged sword.

I would appear normal … until I could walk or talk. I've also learned to plan and improvise.

My biggest asset is to know what I can't do.

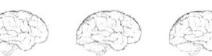

I still didn't have my driving license, so my wife drove me to all my therapies, doctor visits, etc. We stay close to a beach. So, she would often drive me there in the evening, just before the sunset. We do that even now, the only difference being that I'm behind the wheel now.

In the early days, after I came home, she would also shower me.

We had placed a small wooden bench in our bathroom. She would put two legs of the bench outside the shower area while two were inside. Using my walker, I would lower myself on one end of the bench that was outside and slide myself into the shower. It was a very narrow and flimsy bench with hollow aluminum legs. It would creak under my weight. I always feared that one day, it would collapse. To add to my fear, it didn't have a backrest; hence, I would always have the fear of falling.

One day, while doing so, I missed the bench seat and fell to the floor.

Her eyes widened as she clasped her hands on her mouth. "Oh, no!"

"I'm okay," I said.

Adrenaline pumped through my body, and my breathing quickened. I held the edge of the seat and heaved myself up, and, unsteadily, I clambered back on the bench. I waited a few seconds to get my bearings. I steadied myself. I flexed my limbs to check for any bruises, pain, or broken bones. Everything seemed intact.

As she checked my body for any bleeding, her expression changed from a look of concern to relief. "Are you okay?"

I nodded.

Once I knew I was fine, I smiled. "That was a close one."

"Be careful next time, and don't hurry. Get your footing before you shift. You scared me."

I could see the concern in her eyes. I slid myself into the shower. The water was already on. She handed me the shower head and started to lather my back.

I'm writing this minor detail as I genuinely believe such episodes happen. Don't let them deject you. Do not, I repeat, do not feel sorry for yourself. Shrug it off, think of it merely as an episode, and move on. Do not delve into it. The more you think about it, the less confident you'll be in the future. Over time, when you look back at these events, you will realize how far you have come.

My rehab physician, Dr. Adams, closely monitored my progress. He was my go-to doctor for all my queries. If I had any questions, I would ask his guidance.

"Stay away from alcoholic drinks," he told me one day.

I was surprised by his suggestion. I wasn't a regular drinker, but being told that it was prohibited made me want it more.

"Why?" I asked.

"It's not good for you in your condition. It'll impact your balance even further."

"So, stop drinking forever?"

"Start with one year of no alcohol and then ease into drinks having low alcoholic content, something like a light beer."

"What about hard liquors like whiskey, rum, vodka, etc.?"

"I'd prefer that you don't consume them for the rest of your life, but I don't want to scare you. So, play it by the ear. See how you feel. Don't go overboard. Listen to your body."

I nodded. I was relieved as I prefer beer to other drinks.

Thus, one more restriction was imposed on me—not that I had many to begin with. However, this wasn't something that bothered me so much, as I was more of a social drinker. In fact, I consider myself fortunate that I don't have to consume any medication for the rest of my life. Even after so many years, I am pretty much free of medicines—apart from daily supplements.

I try to eat healthily, less and early, feed my mind by reading, exercise regularly, sleep well, etc. These good habits have rewarded me well.

As I sometimes joke, I'm the fittest sick person. Once, when a nurse was taking my pulse, she looked at me and asked, "Do you go to the gym regularly?"

I was surprised by her question.

"Yes, I try to go thrice per week. Why? How can you tell?"

"Your resting heart rate is low."

I felt good at that moment, but the thing that really terrified me was narrow spaces: MRIs, closed rooms, etc.

Although I would dread the days I had to do an MRI scan, I had no choice. Going inside the narrow tube was a nightmare. Fortunately, as I said before, Xanax helped me a lot. I would take one before the procedure. It helped me relax and put my fears at ease.

I wish science had invented a helmet-like device that could act as an MRI scanner. I'm sure it can be done. All that is needed is some bright scientists and good funding.

Apart from the dreaded MRI tube, I still feel claustrophobic in small spaces—airplanes, closed rooms, etc.

I've made several trips to India and other countries. The most challenging and tedious has been the flight to India. If you look at the map of the world on a globe, Mumbai, India is located precisely at a polar opposite of Los Angeles. There is a twelve-hour difference between the two cities. If it's day here, it's night there.

Again, I digress.

After a few months of staying, my parents flew back, and my in-laws came over. They, too, were of great help. I could see my wife relaxing a little, subconsciously feeling more at ease with her parents.

***

Getting my license

By now, you know how much I enjoyed driving. However, there was a minor problem—well, by minor, I mean a major one. You see, my dear reader, since my license was suspended, I would break the law if I drove. Besides, after the stroke, my reflexes were slow. Hence, without proper training, I would endanger my life and those brave enough to ride with me.

I had to get my license back.

Driving is one of my favorite activities. Like most Californians, I love to drive. To me, it symbolizes freedom. I often drive along the Pacific Coast Highway, flanked by the mighty Pacific Ocean and gentle mountains, the road snaking through them. And the drive was more romantic when it drizzled. The dark clouds over the horizon, the wet roads with traffic lights reflecting on them, the dull mountains, the pitter-patter of raindrops gently hitting the windshield, people enjoying hot beverages in a cozy cafe, etc. All these things put together made one hell of a drive.

I called the DMV office. A male voice answered after being kept on hold for a long time.

"Thank you for calling DMV. How may I assist you?"

"H-hi," I stammered. I wasn't too sure how to converse cohesively. I still was unsure of my speech.

"Hi," he said, sensing my hesitation. "How may I assist you today?" he repeated, his voice softened this time.

"I need my license back," I exclaimed.

"What do you mean 'back'?"

I explained the situation while he patiently listened.

"Hello? Are you there?" I thought I had lost him.

"Yes, I'm still here."

"So, I want to know how to get it back."

"Can I put you on a brief hold while I look up something?"

"Sure."

He put me on hold, and his voice replaced by music. After listening to it for a few minutes, he was back.

"I'm back. Do you have a pencil?"

"Yes."

"Jot this address down."

I shabbily wrote it down in big letters—I was still struggling with my writing.

"What is it?"

"It's our office where cases like yours are handled. It's not crowded like a typical DMV office. You have to go there for a driving test. Once they evaluate you, they'll make a determination. I will also send an official letter with the address and the phone number. Call them to make an appointment."

"Will do. Thank you so much. You have been very helpful. Have a great day."

"You are most welcome. Is there anything else I can assist you with today?"

"No, thank you."

"Sure, and good luck."

After a few days, the letter arrived. I hurriedly tore it open, scanned through it, and called the number to make an appointment. The next available appointment was after two weeks. Now, all I had to do was to wait patiently. Time seemed to move at a snail's pace. Two weeks were way too long. It seemed like two months—not that I had any choice. Moreover, it wasn't like I could practice to refresh my skills.

"Don't you want to practice?" my wife asked.

"Yes," I replied curtly, "but how?"

"We can go for a drive with you—" she said, stopping as she realized what it meant.

"Exactly," I scoffed. "I can't drive. I'll be breaking the law. God forbid, if the CHP pulls us over while I'm behind the wheel, the officer will immediately know that my license is suspended. I've come so close to getting it back. I can't blow my chances now by risking it."

Thankfully, she immediately agreed.

On the day of the appointment, my wife drove me there.

"Nervous?" she asked me on our way.

"Not really," I answered, trying to appear confident, but I was a little apprehensive. of the outcome. My whole life hinged on their decision. If I passed the test, I was free. However, if I didn't, my future was unknown. I'd have to depend upon others driving me around.

The DMV office was located on the first floor—the ground floor in India. As I entered, I was surprised. It looked more like a doctor's office than a DMV office. There was a waiting area with comfy chairs along its walls, and a painting hung above it. It displayed the California coast with the mighty Pacific on one side, jagged mountains on the other, and the Pacific Coast Highway (PCH) snaking through in the middle. On it was a single blue convertible with its top down. I was surprised to see the driver's seat empty. Then my eyes fell on the line below it. It said, 'You can be here, too'. A small table lay in the center with old magazines neatly piled in on it.

On the far right was a brightly lit counter. A young female was sitting behind it, busy looking at her computer screen. Behind her was a vast room with several cubicles, some of which displayed crowns of employees as they worked.

I approached the counter.

She looked up. "Yes?"

I handed her the letter.

She took it and scanned it. Upon confirming its contents, she looked me up on the computer. When she found my records, she nodded. "Take a seat, Mr. Aithal. Someone will be right with you."

I joined my wife, who was flipping through a magazine.

I noticed that we two were the only occupants. After a short while, an old lady entered the office. She appeared to be in her seventies. She was frail with white hair. She held a cane to assist her in walking. I noticed that her free hand, which didn't have the cane, was shaking slightly with tremors, and so was her head. It was apparent she was in no condition to get behind the wheel. Gingerly, she walked to the counter.

"Yes? How can I help you?" the young lady asked her.

The older woman stood still for a while, an expression of sorrow spreading across her face.

I was curious now. *What does she want? What is she doing?*

She slowly reached into her purse, took out a wallet, flipped it open, and removed a card. She looked at it in anguish and hesitantly handed it to the lady.

I was very curious now. My eyes were on the card now. *What is she handling?* I was slightly taken aback when I recognized it.

She had come to surrender her license. She held it tightly between her fingers, not wanting to let it go.

The young woman tugged at it with little force.

I looked at the old lady's face. I could see her sad expression like she was giving up her freedom. I could see the agony in it. She must have driven for years—not just for pleasure but also to run her daily chores.

I witnessed one of the saddest scenes in real life.

Eventually, she left with a defeated stride.

Soon, a young girl entered. She must have been in her late teens or early twenties. She had puffy eyes and a glum expression. She must have been crying. She went to the counter and gave her name. The teenager handed her a letter. The young woman looked at it and tapped the keyboard.

"Wait here, I'll be back," she said, getting up from her chair. Momentarily, she returned with her supervisor.

"Miss Brown?" he asked.

"Yes," she said, nodding and faking a meek smile.

"What seems to be the problem? You know your license has already been suspended for a year, right?"

"Yes, I know that. But I was hoping you'd make an exception. Please." She was begging now.

However, her plea seemed to have no impact on the man. He appeared to have handled hundreds of such cases.

"I'm sorry," the man said, shaking his head. "One year."

The teenager burst into tears. Her shoulder started heaving with sobs.

"Don't do this. I've to drive to attend my classes, I've to drive to take my grandmother for a doctor's visit, I've to drive to—."

"I understand. Let me stop you there. I'm sorry, but you are not getting your license back."

"*Please*," she begged again, her voice becoming a low shriek. "Don't do this."

But her pleas had no impact on the man. He shrugged, turned around, and walked away. She stood there crying for a while and then exited the office.

I was shaken. I started to feel low. I felt my chances of getting my license back evaporating.

My wife squeezed my shaking hands to reassure me. "It'll be fine," she mouthed.

"Mr. Aithal?" the woman shouted.

"Yes," I replied as I got up and slowly approached the counter. Suddenly, an obese lady with a stern face appeared behind her.

"He's all yours, Martha," the woman said, handing her a piece of paper. She scanned it for a few seconds.

"Go to your car," she finally said. "I'll meet you there. What color is it?"

"It's a white Toyota minivan."

Although my wife must have said, "All the best," I didn't hear her. I took a deep breath, got up, and walked towards the door. I was collecting my thoughts. After all, it had been a while since I had gotten behind the wheel. Self-doubt was creeping in. *P, R, N, and D*, I murmured under my breath. Thankfully, I had an automatic, and my right side was coordinated. I would only need the right hand and leg to operate a vehicle.

> There was no way I could have driven a stick shift. It required using my left leg to depress the clutch and would pose a formidable challenge if my vehicle was going on a slope. Back in India, I have only driven stick-shift, and the experience has been horrible on a hill. I would pray that my car would not stop on a slope, but it always did. I've described my experience in my other memoir[5].

In the morning, before driving to the DMV office, I sat behind the wheel—for the first time after a long time, to refamiliarize myself with the location of all the knobs, gadgets, switches, etc.—the feel of the steering wheel in my grips. Now, I hoped that I remembered them all.

---

[5] See amazon.com/dp/B0BHTZ6WYZ

As they say, practice makes one perfect. However, I didn't have a chance to practice my skills. I was going in with my past knowledge and hoped that they weren't rusty.

"Don't overthink," my wife had said. "It's like riding a bicycle. Once you've ridden it, you'll never forget."

"Right," I had grunted sarcastically. "Easy for you to say. Try riding it with only one side functioning."

But now, it didn't matter. My fate would be decided in the next hour. I shook the thought from my mind. The receptionist was watching me. I could feel her eyes upon me. *Does she have the authority to report me? The way I walk? What if she informs someone that I should not get behind the wheel?* Doubtful thoughts made me more nervous. I made an exaggerated effort to walk with confidence. I looked at her and smiled. She smiled back and went back to the screen.

Phew! I was relieved. It was all in my mind. She was just curious.

Gingerly, I went to my car, unlocked it with the key fob, and waited for Martha to appear. After a few seconds, a door adjacent to the door I had exited swung open, and she wobbled towards me. She had a clipboard tucked under her arm.

"Hi," I said, desperately trying to sound cheerful. Before my stroke, people found me charming. I hoped that I still had it in me. My fate was in her hands. She would pass me if she deemed me fit to drive. If not, I'd have to redo it.

"Hi," she said, nodding back sternly, not smiling. She seemed to be a tough cookie. It was obvious that she had encountered many such people who would smile to get their work done. My charm wouldn't work. She was a seasoned professional. I realized she would grade me purely on my performance, not how I smiled or looked.

"Are you ready, sir?"

I nodded. She double-checked her clipboard to ensure that everything was in order. She then looked up at me and nodded.

I swung open the door and slid behind the wheel. The passenger's side door opened, and she clambered in clumsily. She was already out of breath after a short walk. She then buckled herself around her enormous belly and checked to see if I had done the same. I had already buckled myself. She slid the pencil from the top of the clipboard and checked a box. She replaced it on top of her clipboard and looked at me.

I found the ignition, inserted the key, and turned on the engine. I adjusted the rear-view and the side-view mirrors to my liking, ensuring she noticed me doing so. She grunted in approval. I fussed around with the knobs for a few seconds.

"Let's go," she instructed impatiently.

I stopped fiddling.

This is it, I thought. I had done everything possible for me to get to this stage. Everything depended upon my performance now. There was nothing more I could do. My fate was now in her hands. The following minutes would determine my destiny: to be free or to depend on others.

I shifted the gear to R and slowly backed up, remembering to look in my rearview mirror and twist my torso to look back. She unhooked the pencil again and checked a box on the clipboard. *So far, so good,* I thought.

> Dear reader, as you can imagine, driving under scrutiny adds extra pressure. It's one thing if you are driving for pleasure, but a whole other thing when you are being tested when you have to follow each and every rule of the road. I'm sure that you have broken one rule (at least) while driving.

I drove through the parking lot—making sure that my speed limit was well below five—and stopped at the stop sign near the sidewalk. After ensuring that there were no pedestrians, I inched the vehicle to enter the surface street. I looked on both sides to ensure no oncoming cars were on my side of the road. From the corner of my eyes, I noticed her closely observing me. She had her pencil ready, hovering above a box. She checked it as I turned.

One more feather in my cap, I thought, as my confidence was growing.

"Take a right."

I turned onto the surface street and slowly increased my speed, keeping an eye on the speedometer to ensure I wasn't driving above the posted speed limit. She craned her neck to see my speedometer and checked a box. *Good.*

I slowed near the first intersection to look on either side for oncoming vehicles. Under normal circumstances, I would keep driving without looking on either side. However, I had read that the instructors graded you on that, too. She ticked one more checkbox.

I smiled to myself. My confidence was growing. I was doing good.

The vehicle stopped at the next light. When the light turned green, I gently began to drive ahead.

"Not straight. Take the ramp."

My heart sank. We were going to drive on the freeway, which I had done innumerable times in the past. However, this was different. I was going to be tested to see if I was fit to drive on the freeway. I remember my very first time driving on the freeway in the U.S. when I was in my twenties. My friend, who had driven on the U.S. freeways, sat beside me.

"Remember one thing. Driving on the freeway is very easy. However, the trickiest part is entering it," he had said.

I steeled myself and turned the minivan to get on the on-ramp. The freeway meter was on, helping control the merging vehicles. The light turned green. I stopped at the light and eagerly looked at it to turn green.

> Dear reader, if you have ever driven on the U.S. freeways, you know how I must have felt. You feel you are on a racetrack and waiting for the 'go' signal.

It was my turn to merge. My pulse quickened. I started to breathe heavily. I pressed the gas pedal, but my vehicle was too slow to merge with the other speeding cars. I found it difficult to merge with the traffic. I froze. Cars started to honk behind me. The ones that passed me gave me a dirty look—or mouthed cuss words. Sweat began to form on my forehead and run down my nose.

"Sir, are you ok?"

I nodded, but it was indisputable that I was not. Fortunately, the right-most lane was for exiting the freeway only.

"Don't get on the freeway. Take the next exit, but slowly. Watch out for other vehicles that may want to exit."

Her face had hardened, and she vigorously scratched an X on the clipboard.

I obeyed her. Within a few minutes, we were back in the parking lot. She didn't even wait for me to turn off the engine. She quickly unbuckled and exited the vehicle. I followed her.

"Well?" I asked, even though I knew her answer. I would have to go through it again.

"Well, Mr. Aithal," she said, looking at me sternly, "you are not ready to drive yet."

Obviously, I thought. I had to mitigate my disastrous performance.

"Okay. So, should I take my next appointment?"

"No," she said, "that won't be necessary."

"What do you mean?" I was alarmed.

"We will send you a letter telling you what to do next."

"Oh, okay." Although I knew I had to redo it, I told myself it didn't sound so bad.

As I entered the DMV office, my wife looked up from her magazine with a hopeful expression. However, I didn't have to tell her the result. One look at my glum face told her everything.

"Don't worry," she said on our way back. "We'll try again."

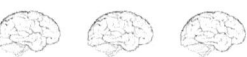

I eagerly waited for a mail from the DMV. I could see the mailbox from my office. Every afternoon, I'd wait for the mailman to deliver. Fearing that I might have missed him, I would annoy my wife.

"Did the mail come? Can you go check the mailbox?"

She would roll her eyes and entertain me. Sometimes, she would return with a stack of envelopes—mostly junk mail and often empty-handed. This went on for about two weeks. The waiting was agonizing.

Finally, it arrived. When my wife gave me the stack of mail, I quickly sifted through them to see the sender's address. Upon seeing the DMV, I tore open the thin envelope. My eyes quickly started to scan the words.

Suddenly, my eyes stopped at a single word: REVOKED. I was confused. *Revoked?!!* What did it mean? I knew that my license had been suspended, but this? Revoked? It must have been a mistake, a clerical error. I reread the letter, hoping the word would mean something else. I flipped the paper to look at its back to see if there was some explanation. There was none.

"Revoked?" I asked my wife, not realizing that my voice had raised a few decibels. "What does it mean?"

I was confused. I thought the letter would mention the date of my next appointment, but this word had a finality.

The finality of this single word sounded like a prison sentence. It felt as if my freedom had been snatched away.

She looked at me sorrowfully as she realized what it meant. I, however, could not accept that I would not be allowed to drive for the rest of my life. The logical part of my brain knew what the word meant, but the emotional part refused to accept it.

I would not be able to go for long drives, take road trips, or rent cars; I would not be able to use my driver's license as proof of residence or photo ID. There were innumerable things I wouldn't be able to do.

Noticing my dark expression, my wife extended a hand. "Let me read it." She frowned as she read the letter, but her eyes brightened when she reached the bottom. She showed it to me. "Look here. It says that you can call this number to appeal their decision."

I didn't reply. I was preoccupied with my sorrow. She gently shook me by my shoulders.

"Hey," she said, "look at me. It'll be fine. Let me call them."

Slowly, I looked up at her. I weakly nodded, but I had very little hope.

She dialed the number. She cocked her head to hold the receiver between her head and her collarbone while it was ringing. When someone answered it, she straightened her head and held the receiver with her other hand.

"Hello," she said, "I have a reference number." She took the letter and read it aloud.

"That's right," she confirmed. "I understand what it says, but all I need is an appointment to see someone to plead my case."

I could hear muffled sounds as the opposite person spoke.

"Yes…yes," she said, nodding as she wrote on the letter.

"Thank you so much," she finally said, smiling as she disconnected. Looking at her expression, I knew she had something good to say. However, I was apprehensive.

"Good news," she said.

"What?" I looked at her suspiciously.

"We have an appointment."

My eyes brightened slightly.

"Really?" I had expected something different. However, it was good news indeed. *What did you expect? To have your decision overturned by a call?* I admonished myself. *Be real.*

"Yes," she said, nodding, "but the only thing is that they want to see our medical records."

"Oh, why?"

"I don't know, but this is good news. Now cheer up."

My spirits lifted, but I had a nagging feeling about them wanting to look at my medical records. What were they looking for? Even though I had not gone through them thoroughly.

On one hand, it was good news, but on the other, it was worrisome.

As my appointment day neared, I became more anxious. I started mentally preparing myself for how I would conduct myself.

"So, Mr. Aithal, tell us why we should give you your license back?"

"I wasn't given a proper chance the first time…no…I think I deserve a second chance…no…I want to be retested…no, no, no."

I had many such internal dialogs. Many times, I'd catch myself mouthing them. I'd then look around to see nobody had noticed me, fearing that they would think I was losing my mind.

Finally, it was the day of our appointment. We drove south to the same DMV office, where the same young receptionist behind the counter greeted us.

She smiled as she recognized me. "Hi."

I handed her the letter and informed her I was there for my appointment. She typed on the keyboard to confirm it and spoke to someone in the back office.

"Take a seat," she informed me as she replaced the receiver, "Someone will be right with you."

I waited with a held breath, praying it would not be the same lady who had failed me. This was the moment. My freedom hinged upon their decision. In the next few minutes, my life could change forever.

My wife held my hand and squeezed it. I looked at her nervously.

"Relax," she whispered.

I nodded, smiling weekly. I wasn't feeling as confident as she was. The room was silent except for the ticking of the wall clock, the faint ring of a phone somewhere in the back office, and the clicking of the keyboard as the receptionist typed.

Momentarily, the door next to the counter opened. A woman in her mid-thirties walked out. She wore a navy business suit. She had an oval face and piercing brown eyes.

"Mr. Aithal?" she asked.

I got up. "Yes."

She approached me and proffered her hand. "Hello, I'm Sandy." She dimpled as she smiled.

"Hello." I said, shaking her hand.

"Follow me," she said, walking towards the far side of the waiting area and opening a door.

"Can my wife join us?"

"Of course," she said as she held the door open for me.

We both followed her. She flicked a switch on the wall, and the ceiling lights flickered to life.

It was a relatively large room that was unused. It had empty cubicles on the far side and a large table in the front with few chairs around it. It was their conference area.

She sat on one of the chairs. "Have a seat." She gestured to do the same. She had the letter in her hand. She read it slowly and looked at me.

"Your license has been revoked. We have already deemed you not fit to drive on the road."

"Yes, I know that."

"Not only will you endanger your life, but other drivers, too."

"I understand that. I'm not here for that. I do not expect you to give me my license back."

She raised her eyebrows. "Then, why are you here?"

I leaned forward as I lowered my voice. "All I'm asking is that you test me again. After that, if you still feel the same way, I will accept your decision."

She frowned as she thought for a second.

"Please," I pleaded. "Just give me one more chance. *Please.*"

The clock on the wall ticked as she contemplated her decision. She reread the letter and looked at me. My fate hinged on her decision, and it was evident that she was not taking it lightly.

"Let me go through your records." She reached for my medical file on the table, opened it, and started to read the reports. I sat silently while she carefully read through them, hoping nothing would raise a red flag.

Suddenly, her eyes narrowed. She leaned forward to reread the sentence. She looked up at me.

"It says here that your memory could be impacted."

I was confused. "Huh?" My memory was intact. *What have they written? The doctors have tested me many times. Not once did they or anyone else say anything about my memory. What now?* I thought desperately. I leaned forward, and she turned the file to me. She pointed to a sentence.

"Look here. It clearly states that."

As I read the sentence, my heart sank. It said that the brain injury could affect my memory. I felt my world collapsing. I looked at her pleadingly.

"*Could.*" I suddenly said.

"Excuse me?"

"It says *could*, not *will*," I said, emphasizing the two words. "It says it could affect my memory and not will impact it."

With a frown, she reread the line. "Hmm." She looked up.

She saw my sorrowful face. Although she felt sorry for me, she had to do her job. "I'm sorry, Mr. Aithal. I can't let you behind the wheel."

I felt the ground opening under me. My chances of ever driving seem to be quickly fading.

She looked at my face. She realized the power she had over me. She could change my life. She fell silent for a while, continuing to read the file.

"But," she finally said, looking up.

"But?" I asked hopefully. *Is there a chance?*

"You definitely can not reappear for a driving test without a written test. Getting your license back involves recognizing and understanding all the signs."

"Of course," I said, nodding enthusiastically as a glimmer of hope lifted my spirits. Suddenly, I saw a faint light at the end of a dark tunnel.

"I'm willing to take a written test," I said, confident about my mental capabilities.

She studied the file, deciding whether to allow me to take one. Finally, her expression changed as she had made up her mind.

"Okay," she wrote down a date and time on paper. "This is your appointment for the written test. Once you pass that, we will give you an appointment for the road test."

I smiled. "Thank you."

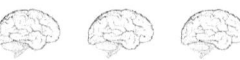

I now saw a way to my freedom. I started to study the driver's handbook. Although I had been driving on U.S. roads for a long time, I realized how nuanced the laws could be.

The test was going to be a multiple-choice question. However, I knew that the choices could confuse me. For example, if you are about to make a left turn, you must signal continuously during the last ____ feet before the turn. A: 50, B:75, or C:100, or one of the questions would show a sign and ask me to identify it. The tests are designed for one to be able to drive safely to themselves, other vehicles, and pedestrians.

However, I was not intimidated even though the book was over eighty pages. Reading is one of my favorite activities; moreover, I can retain knowledge. I was very confident about my mental faculties.

I returned to the DMV office on the day of my appointment. The same lady greeted me, took me to the empty office area, and handed me the test paper.

"You have thirty minutes to complete the test," she informed me.

"Only thirty?" I was surprised, "I thought it was usually for sixty minutes."

"Yes," she said, nodding, "But if you look at the test paper, you'll notice that it has half the number of questions we usually ask."

"Oh." I looked at my test paper. "Right."

"Good luck," she said as she checked the wall clock to ensure it synced with her wristwatch.

I sat at the conference table and concentrated on the questionnaire. Soon, I was immersed in it, rereading the questions before selecting the correct option. After scratching the option to the last question, I looked at the clock. I had five more minutes left before my time was up; *enough time to recheck my answers*. I flipped to the first page and started to read my responses. I had been correct the first time around. I was feeling confident. I heard footsteps muffled by the carpet as I read my last answer. The woman appeared.

"Done?"

"Yes," I said, handing her my test paper.

"I'll be back," she said, perusing my answers. She reappeared momentarily. I looked at her face, eagerly trying to decipher her expression.

"Well?" I exclaimed.

She smiled. "Congratulations, Mr. Aithal. You passed."

"Alright," I said and air-fisted with joy. I felt as if a heavy burden had been lifted off my shoulders. After a few minutes of euphoria, I was curious about how I had performed.

"How many did I get wrong?"

"None. You answered all of them correctly."

See, I told you my memory is intact, I wanted to say.

"Wow. That's great to hear," I said instead, feeling exuberant. It isn't easy to describe how I felt at the moment. A sense of achievement? One hurdle overcome, one more to go?

I felt my life getting back on track after a long struggle. Even though I knew I had a long way to go, I thought I had taken a step in the right direction.

The lady was satisfied with my ability to decipher various rules and signs. I was granted a temporary license with the condition that I attend a driving school. Also, this was not a regular school. I had to go to a school that specializes in training people with my condition. It had to be attached to a hospital. She gave me a number to call to make an appointment.

The following morning, I called them.

"Hello," said a cheerful voice. "Thank you for calling the La Palma Hospital. How may I direct your call?"

Hospital? I must have misdialed. I hung up and redialed. The same cheerful lady answered.

"Hello. Thank you for calling the La Palma Hospital. How may I direct your call?"

"H—hello?" I hesitated.

"Yes?"

"Have I dialed the right number?" I read out the number aloud.

"That's correct, sir. You have reached the right number. Which department are you looking for?"

"I'm not sure. The DMV gave me this number."

"Ah," the lady exclaimed. "You want the driving school. One moment, please."

Before I could ask her further, I heard the pipe music. She had put me on hold.

After a little while, a gruff voice answered. "Hello?"

"Yes, hello," I leaned forward from my chair. "I need an appointment."

"For?"

"Driving, of course."

The man remained silent for a few seconds. I thought he had disconnected.

"Hello? Are you still there?"

"Yes, I'm here," he said in a smirking voice.

"Well?"

"You can't just make an appointment over the phone, that too, only for one driving session."

"Then?"

"You will need to book at least ten sessions."

Ten? I was surprised. I had not even taken ten sessions for the first time.

"How long does each session last?"

"For an hour."

"Fine," I mumbled. I booked appointments for ten sessions. The man informed me that my first session would be for ninety minutes.

"You have to fill in some paperwork first, and then you have to familiarize yourself with the car you'll be driving," he explained. "Be here on time."

Before I could thank him, he had disconnected.

The driving school was located in a building across from La Palma Hospital. I—along with my wife—took the elevator up to the third floor. The door at the end of a well-lit hallway displayed a board that said, 'La Palma Hospital Driving School.' I entered the room and went to the receptionist. I informed her that I was there for my appointment.

After looking me up, she picked up the phone.

"Hi, it's me. Your 10:30 is here. Yes, I know it's only ten o'clock. He has to fill in the paperwork."

She handed me a clipboard and a pen without looking at me.

"Yes, I know," she continued, "I just handed it to him. I'll call you when he's done."

After replacing the phone, she looked at me and said, "Fill this in."

I nodded, took a seat, and started filling in the paperwork. When I was done, I walked over to the counter and handed it to the lady.

She nodded in approval as she scanned it. Once she was satisfied that everything was in order, she picked up the phone again to call the instructor.

"He'll be right with you," she said, smiling as she replaced the receiver.

Momentarily, the door next to the counter opened. A bespectacled, curly-haired man in his late forties or early fifties greeted me. He had a slight belly. He wore gray pants and a tee that was a size smaller. He had muscular arms.

"Hi, I'm Tom," he said, smiling. "I'm your instructor. I'll be retraining you."

Retraining. The word stung like a bee. It was apparent that he was used to seeing people like me.

"Hi, Tom," I reciprocated, shaking his hand.

"Follow me."

He led me to the parking lot to a blue Cadillac. It looked long and intimidating. I'm used to driving smaller vehicles that maneuver much more quickly through traffic.

Also, they are much easier to park. And to add to the challenge, it had been ages since I drove a sedan. I'm used to driving SUVs and minivans. *How am I going to drive this monster?* I thought.

Besides, it was much lower than the SUV that I was used to. Getting in and out would be a challenge for someone in my condition.

Gingerly, I walked to the driver's side door, unlocked it, and carefully lowered myself. Tom sat in the passenger's side seat. I looked around to familiarize myself with the controls.

I immediately noted that this vehicle was very different. It was fitted with various gadgets to accommodate those with special needs.

In addition to my brakes and gas pedals, he, too, had a pair on his side. The steering wheel was modified, too. A thin rod with a lever protruded on its side and ran vertically. It connected to the brakes and the gas pedals. It was meant for someone with difficulty with lower limbs. Fortunately, I would not have to use them.

Suddenly, he opened the glove box and started to rummage through it.

"Where is it?" he murmured under his breath.

"Aha." His eyes brightened as he felt it. Like a magician, he pulled out a balled fist and opened it before me to reveal its content. My eyes narrowed in confusion. I wasn't sure what I was looking at. It was a circular knob that looked like a tiny mushroom made out of steel with threads on the tapering end. I looked at it, still confused.

"What is it?"

"This will help you drive," he said as he proceeded to screw it in the hole on my steering wheel. "You won't have to hold the steering with both hands while turning the vehicle. All you have to do is to hold the knob and use it to rotate the steering with a single hand."

I looked at the tiny little object—now mounted on the steering.

"No," I said, shaking my head.

"No?" His eyebrows furrowed in confusion. "What do you mean?"

"No," I repeated, a more loudly this time. I shook my head as if this object that would assist me was my nemesis.

I wanted to be able to drive any vehicle without the need for specialized gadgets attached to it.

This little knob symbolized me being dependent. It would be a constant reminder that there was something wrong with me.

"I don't want any gadgets," I said resolutely. "I want to be able to drive a regular vehicle, any vehicle." I didn't realize that my voice had risen a few decibels.

Tom looked at me in surprise for a few seconds. He saw the resolve on my face.

"Oh, I see. Interesting," he finally said, and then he shrugged. "Well, anyways, if you need it, it's there for you."

"Please take it off."

"You sure?"

"Yes."

"Okay, as you wish." He shrugged again as he unscrewed it.

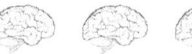

I trained (or retrained) hard, driving through windy roads, going on the freeway, navigating through traffic, parking, and reversing.

Tom saw that I was a seasoned driver who just needed to repolish his skills. He began relaxing after a while. He would be instructing me gently. And sometimes he would just give me subtle hints by his actions. For example, if I forgot to turn on the knob to indicate that I wanted to turn, he would crane his neck and cup his ear to tell me that he couldn't hear the rhythmic ticking sound of the turn indicator.

Finally, I was ready for the driving test (well, as ready as I could be). On the day of my driving test, I was a nervous wreck. Fortunately, I had a different examiner this time. However, he, too, was closely observing me. I slowed down at every intersection and looked both ways (in an exaggerated motion for his benefit). When I pulled my car into the parking lot and parked it, I was pleased with my performance. He turned to me and said three magical words I had been thirsting to hear for a long time.

"You have passed."

Chapter 5

Therapies continued/surprise party

MY CONFIDENCE LEVEL GREW ENORMOUSLY after I got my license back. Many were surprised that I had achieved this feat. Needless to say, their astonishment was not misplaced. Getting my license back was the most challenging task in everything I've endured.

Without it, I might as well be bound to a wheelchair. I would end up depending on others to do minor tasks such as going to the stores, the gym, going out, and so many other mundane tasks that we take for granted. On several occasions, I would go for long drives or volunteer to drive my wife to run errands.

On several occasions, I would drive to the beach for fifteen minutes, watch the sunset for five minutes, and drive back. Also, over the years, I've driven many of my friends and family—who have visited us from India—to show L.A. and the rest of California.

When I flew abroad, I could also rent a car and explore locations usually inaccessible by large tour buses.

This was only possible because I had my license back.

> Dear reader, there is a snaking road near where I live. It may be easy to drive on for an average person; however, it is a good training ground for a newbie—or someone who is retrained. When I was being retrained, my instructor always made me drive on that to hone my reflexes. Years later, when my daughter was preparing to get her license, I would always make her drive on that road. I don't know how she felt about it, but it helped immensely while retraining.

I continued my therapies. There is an Olympic-sized community pool located near where I live. It is not just long—like a typical Olympic pool—but also wide. It's divided into three sections. The first section is only five feet deep, so little children learn to swim there. The second section is slightly deeper, with multiple lanes. It is for lap swimmers. The third section is the deepest, with a high diving board. It's meant for those who want to practice diving. Divers with lithe bodies would spring up and down, somersault while cocooning in a ball, and stretch their bodies straight like arrows just before breaking the water's surface. It was a sight to behold.

The first section was perfect for me. I would be able to wade long distances unencumbered. However, I would have to go very early in the morning before the pool started getting crowded before the regular classes started. This would hinder my wading as I would have to navigate through a crowd instead of walking in a straight line.

Also, this was a public pool open to regular people. People with my condition usually prefer to go to specialized pools closed to the general public. And to make matters more challenging, if I was sitting or standing, people thought nothing was wrong with me. I appeared like any other normal person one would encounter. Thus, wanting to be as normal as possible was a double-edged sword. It would be wrong of me to get any special treatment at my convenience.

However, people are very considerate towards me. When I'm walking, they realize I'm slow and give me personal space, hold the door, listen to me patiently while I'm talking, etc.

Just like the Cal State Long Beach pool, I had to go way early in the morning before the regular classes started. I would get up at five a.m. and drive to the pool. Yes, *I drive to the pool* on my own. My wife would have to drive me if I didn't have my license back. This would have a snowballing impact on our daily lives—dropping my children off to their schools, going grocery shopping to get ready to prepare meals, etc. That was the best time for me as the pool would be empty with few early risers. I would practice walking in the water to gain the confidence to do the same on land.

Later, I also went to a pool at Ability First[6] near where I lived. Fortunately, this was in the evening and was only available to seniors and people with my condition. When I called them, I was informed that I had to obtain a doctor's note to be able to go. This made me feel more confident in my environment. Also, the proximity to the pool was much more approachable than the public pool I had been to earlier, where the parking lot was far away.

Understandably, the public pool was not designed for people with special needs. A lot of thought is needed when building a pool for those with special needs: access, devices

---

[6] To find out more, please visit abilityfirst.org/long-beach-center/

to lower someone with severe disability, floors for better grips, a shower area, etc.

Over the years, I've visited many such facilities: my gym —with a pool—a community pool, specialized pools, therapy pools, etc. Yes, it gets overwhelming sometimes, but the desire to get better and the determination to lead an everyday life have kept me going.

After all, what choices did I have? I remembered the famous dialog from Apollo 13: *Failure is not an option.*

One year of my recovery was approaching.

"What do you want to do?" my wife asked me.

"Nothing special," I replied. "Maybe go out to a restaurant and have a beer."

As Dr. Adams had advised, I had refrained from drinking for a year. Although I had not missed it, I looked forward to having a chilled one.

"Okay," she said, nodding.

Soon, I forgot about the plan. On my first anniversary, she said we would be going over to our friend's house for dinner.

I was surprised when she volunteered to drive. Usually, it was something I'd be doing. When we reached their house, I commented about her punctuality, which was unlike her. We greeted our friends at the door. We walked through the unlit living room to the family-room-cum-kitchen. I could only see the family room from the living room as the living room wall obscures my view of the kitchen area. The family room was dimly lit. A basketball game was on TV.

"Let's watch a game," the husband said.

"Sure, who's playing?"

"Lakers," he replied.

I began to walk towards their couch.

"*Surprise.*" The chorus startled me. My eyes widened. I jerked my head towards the noise. I was taken aback. It took me a few seconds for my mind to catch up with my eyes—what I was witnessing.

I saw the smiling faces of my friends. But how could it be? They didn't even know the hosts. I'm used to seeing them in different environments. This was a scene out of sync. My brain wasn't computing. Also, to add to my confusion, I saw a face I had not seen in years. He was a good friend of mine who resided in New York. To see him among my other friends further confused me.

Before I could react normally, my wife wrapped her hands around me and hugged me.

"Surprise," she whispered.

I was speechless for a while.

"H—how? W—when?" I stammered. My brain was coming back to normalcy. I was able to think logically.

Of course, Clue#1:She is punctual. Clue#2: She is volunteering to drive. You should have known better.

My New York friend handed me a can of beer.

"Cheers," he said, taking a swig from his can.

"Cheers," I raised my can, brought it to my lips, and closed my eyes, savoring the cold, golden liquid swirling in my mouth. It was pure heaven.

When I opened my eyes, I noticed everyone watching me, waiting to see if there were any side effects.

"Don't worry, guys. I'm fine," I said.

"How does it feel?" one of my friends asked me. I didn't have to reply, as my ecstatic expression conveyed everything.

Since then, I've had alcoholic beverages several times; however, the feeling can't be recreated. To appreciate what you are missing, you must give it up for a while.

> Dear reader, although what I gave up is remarkable, it pales compared to what my wife

gave up for ten years. Yes, she voluntarily gave up chocolate for ten years to show solidarity.

The surprise party continued until late. Eventually, we bid our friends goodnight and profusely thanked our hosts.

I wanted to drive on our way back, but my wife insisted on driving me. Although I had just one drink, she was concerned about the impact the alcohol would have. Of course, she was right. I had worked so hard to get my license back. I didn't want to lose it again for my stubbornness. If the CHP pulled me over for any reason—not just related to alcohol, it would be curtains for me. They would make me walk a straight line, which I could not do.

It was and still is very important to constantly remind myself of my shortcomings and not to be too adventurous.

India visit for the first time

The first time I went back to India after my stroke, I stayed there for two months. Having spent the first twenty-five years of my life there, I was looking forward to going to India. I am very familiar with the country and am instantly at ease with my surroundings. Going back has always been a pleasure. However, I was a little apprehensive this time as my condition was different. But my worries evaporated the moment I lay on the familiar faces. My family and my friends had come to receive me. It was wonderful to see them all.

> Dear reader, you can relate to the feeling if you are from India. The moment you step out of the airport, you are greeted by a crown. You eagerly (with a silly grin) scan it until you see familiar faces. In fact, the silly grin starts the moment the plane wheels touch the ground and you are back in your homeland. You spend the rest of your

time visiting many places you frequented in your earlier life.

My father had arranged a stay at an *ashram*, a health retreat at Lonavala (a picturesque and lush green city on the outskirts of Mumbai—where I am from). It was a trendy destination for many Mumbaikars.

He had booked a small apartment in a two-story building. Similar buildings were scattered throughout the vast property. In the center was a hall where all residents gathered thrice daily for their meals.

Outside the dining hall was a vast veranda for them to sit and socialize. It was the monsoon season; thus, many would take their afternoon tea there while it rained outside.

Across from my apartment building was a shed where cows were milked daily in the morning. The farmers would take the fresh milk to the kitchen to boil it into *ghee*—purified butter.

I spent the first few days exploring the property when it was not raining. I would enjoy the crisp, fresh air caressing my face. On the second day, I stumbled upon a smaller structure than others. It didn't look like it housed apartments. Its doors were wide open, inviting me to explore further. I entered gingerly. I looked around in awe.

I was in a massive hall with a thin carpet. Later, I found out that it was prayer-cum-lecture-cum-meditation hall.

During my stay, my family and friends regularly visited me on the weekend—the retreat had a 'no visitors on the weekdays' policy. My father stayed with me for the entire duration, and my wife visited me whenever possible. After all, she, too, needed to be with her family.

One day, I was overjoyed when a friend from the neighboring city of Pune visited me. We had worked together when we were in Florida, and we reminisced about our times there. It was good to see him.

I had settled into a daily routine: go for a walk, go to the dining hall for breakfast, do one of the *kriyas*—therapies prescribed to cleanse my body, rest and recover, go to the dining hall for lunch, do one more *kriya*, rest and recover, go to the dining hall for afternoon tea, socialize with fellow-residents (if you want to), do one more *kriya*, rest and recover, go to the meditation hall, go to the dining hall for dinner, socialize (if you want to), read a little, go to bed.

The apartment did not have a TV. So, I was unaware of what was happening in the outside world. I must say that I was totally cut off from the happenings outside for the first time. It gave me a chance to reflect on life. Also, after the end of my month-long stay, when I reconnected to the world, I realized nothing had changed. It makes one realize how small and insignificant they are in the larger scheme. Did it help me in my recovery? I don't want to dismiss it summarily. So, let me put it mildly. It helped me to shed some weight.

The fresh air, the simple and pure food, and the daily regimen of exercises, ayurvedic practices, massages, etc., helped me a lot. I was weighed on the first and the last day of my stay. I'm proud to say I lost seven kilos in a month (and probably gained it back in the next month).

Upon my return, I stayed at my home for one more month. Every day in the evening, my son, holding a cricket bat in one hand and a tennis ball in the other, would eagerly wait for my brother to return from his office so that they could go out and play. My brother also taught him ride a bicycle.

My son was getting extra attention from everyone. After all, this was the very first-time people in India were seeing him. My daughter, too, went through the same fascination when she met her relatives in India for the first time in 1992. Everyone was pampering her. She was only two and a half years old then, but it was a memorable experience. She may not remember it, but I do.

After a month of being among friends and family, gaining a few pounds of delicious home-cooked meals lovingly prepared by my mother, and eating out at all my favorite restaurants (as I said earlier, I grew up in India and spent the first twenty-five years of my life there), it was time for me to return home.

This was my first time going through the security check in a wheelchair. When I approached the X-ray body scanner, they made me get up and walk through it. Unsteadily, I managed to do that. After going through the scanner, I sighed in relief, thinking my woes were over. How wrong was I!

"Go there," a security officer pointed to my next station just as I was about to sit in the wheelchair. My gaze followed his hand, and my eyes widened in surprise.

A security guard stood near a small wooden stool. He beckoned me and pointed down at the stool.

"Come here and stand up on this."

What?! Is he serious? How am I going to do that? Can't he see I have difficulty walking? I was terrified. Gingerly, I stepped forward. Frantically, I looked around to hold onto something, but no such luck.

There was nothing but the small stool in front of me. My surprise had turned into fear. I put one foot up on the stool. Immediately, I started to sway. Seeing I would lose my balance, the security guard thrust out an arm to help me climb. With great effort, I stood on the narrow stool. I was struggling to stop my knees from buckling. After a few seconds, the security guard let go of my hand. I felt like I was standing on a mountain peak thousands of feet high.

"Lift your hands and spread them," he ordered. He then proceeded to scan my body with a wand. I stood there, unsteadily, waiting for it to get over.

When satisfied, he stamped my boarding pass and helped me climb down. I held his hand, climbed down, and sat in the wheelchair. I exhaled in relief. My fear was rapidly turning into anger. *This is so insane. Why can't they have a special queue for wheelchair-bound travelers? Is this stool for his convenience so he doesn't have to bend?*

I raised my voice. "Excuse me?"

The guard had his back to me. He was already scanning the next passenger. He turned around.

"Yes?"

"What do you do with people with my condition?"

"Nothing," he shrugged. "We help them to climb up the stool."

I realized there was no point in arguing with him. He was just a tiny cog in the big wheel doing his job. He had no power to make a decision. I was just relieved it was over.

It was a traumatic experience. I couldn't help but compare it with the TSA Security Check I did a few months ago. There, at the ticket counter, once I informed them that I required a wheelchair, not once did I have to get up. They patted me down and wanded me in my seat. I was wheeled all the way until I reached the aircraft door.

This has happened each time I have been to India. For any average person, it's not a big deal. They would do it without giving it a second thought. However, for me, it was akin to climbing Mount Everest. Traveling has always been a pleasure for me. However, I now dread the experience. I sincerely pray that no one has to go through this.

Over the years, I've traveled to several countries, and nowhere else have I been subjected to such a traumatic experience. It can not only be fearful but dangerous, too. A person can have a fall and have serious injuries.

As the plane took off the runway, my low spirits gradually evaporated. I was looking forward to my regular life.

However, apart from the jetlag, I always feel the stark difference of how different things are when I've come back from India.

> Dear reader, the strange thing about jetlag is that I never jetlagged when I traveled to India. It only happens on my return. Strange, but true. I'm sure there's a scientific explanation for this.

Just twenty-four hours ago, I was surrounded by many people—my family and friends. The constant cacophony of cars honking, TV blasting, many people talking with raised voices, etc., was replaced by the quietness of life in the U.S.

Suddenly, there were just four of us.

Stereotactic Surgery

Slowly, I settled back into my regular rhythms of U.S. life, and my daily regimen began. I continued my therapies and doctor visits. Whenever they recommended that I get a new MRI scan, although I dreaded it, I powered through it (thank you, Xanax.)

I also went to the Long Beach Memorial for my therapy sessions as an outpatient. I'd pass by the room I was in and shudder at the memories. An army of therapists diligently worked on my gait and coordination. They would make on-the-spot adjustments as they saw fit—*try a cane, walk straight, bend your leg slightly, use your core while walking, etc.* Every time I visited my doctor, he—just like the therapists—would recommend me using a cane. I was hesitant to walk with a cane as I was way too young and not ready for it. However, looking back, I wish I had tried it then.

I was making slow but steady progress. However, one question constantly nagged me: *What if it happened again?* I (or anybody else) could do nothing to prevent it.

You are fine, going about your daily business in one second, and, in another second, *boom*. Your life changes forever.

The most frustrating thing, apart from the physical pain, is the mental agony. I would think of the things I could do *before* my stroke, and although I wanted to do many things, my body wasn't cooperating.

Since then, I have adjusted my thinking to feel better. I would think of my life after the brain injury and how far I have come. Besides, I had to snap out of such gloomy thinking and think of my family around me. After all, I was responsible for them.

We were sitting at the kitchen table one morning, sipping my coffee. Looking out at my backyard, l was lost in thoughts. My wife noticed that I was unusually silent.

"What are you thinking?" she asked.

I lied, as I took a swig. "Nothing."

"C'mon, there is something that is bothering you. I know you too well."

"It's just that…," I trailed off.

"Just what?"

"What if it happens again?"

"What if what happens aga—," she stopped mid-sentence when she realized what I meant.

"Yes, that. What if I get a stroke again?"

She admonished me. "Don't say that."

"I know how you feel, but what if? After all, we have to talk of the worst-case scenario. Only then will we be able to prevent it."

She remained silent for a while, lost in her thoughts.

Now, I felt guilty that I had brought her mood down, too.

"Any suggestions?" I looked at her.

"Why don't you ask Dr. Adams? There may be a treatment to prevent it," she finally said.

"Good idea," I said. My spirits were lifted. I eagerly looked forward to my next appointment, which was two weeks away. I tried changing it to an earlier date, but his receptionist informed me he was booked. She would not be able to change my appointment. I also thought of talking to him over the phone or emailing him.

However, my wife dissuaded me.

"It's just a matter of two weeks. Be patient," she said. "It's better that you ask him in person."

I reluctantly agreed.

For the next two weeks, I tried not to think about it. I tried to divert my mind by watching TV shows, reading, playing with my children, etc. It worked to an extent, but once the thought crept up in my mind, it was impossible to shrug it off until a new thought crept in.

On my next visit, the moment I entered, I blurted out, "Doctor, I need your advice."

"What is it?" He got up from his chair, walked to the door and closed it. He looked at my concerned expression and waited for me to say something. "Well?"

I looked at my wife.

"Go ahead," she said.

I nodded and leaned forward. "What if it happens again?"

"What if what happens again? Oh, your stroke?"

"Yes," I said, nodding. "Is there any treatment to mitigate it?"

He remained silent for a while, thinking. Suddenly, his eyebrows narrowed as he leaned forward to the desk. My medical file lay there. He reached for it and sifted through it. His eyes brightened when he found what he was looking for.

He raised his eyebrows at me. "You had an AVM in the Pons area, right?"

I nodded. "Yes."

Doesn't he know? I thought *He must be handling many such cases, each with a different type of stroke. How can I expect him to remember every case?*

"There might be a way."

"What is it?" I asked him hopefully. I was willing to try anything.

"Stereotactic Surgery."

"Stereo S-surgery?" I stammered. "What is it?" I had never heard of it.

He laughed. "No—no, Stereotactic Surgery."

The word 'surgery' made me shudder. Instruments such as scalpels, scissors, forceps, clamps, needs, etc., started to dance in front of me. A chill ran down my spine.

"Surgery?" I went numb with fear. "They'll open my skull?"

He laughed again. "No. It's not as ominous as it sounds. It's a non-invasive procedure. Nothing drastic like opening your skull. Why don't you look it up? You'll feel much at ease."

"Oh, okay." I felt relieved. "So, which department do I call to make an appointment?"

"Unfortunately, we don't do it at Long Beach Memorial."

"No?" I was surprised. Long Beach Memorial was one of the best and most well-equipped hospitals. "Who does it then?"

"UCLA Medical Center. You'll have to go there."

"Oh," I said, sounding crestfallen. The image of me being in a hospital bed made me shudder. "How long does it take? How many days will I have to stay there?"

"No—no. It's an outpatient surg…er…procedure," he said.

I noticed that he switched the word to lessen its impact.

"You'll go there in the morning and return by the end of day," he continued.

"Oh, really? That's nice!" I exclaimed as my spirits lifted.

He smiled. "Yes, really."

We spent the next thirty minutes reviewing my progress. He meticulously recorded it.

I also informed him about my driving.

"That's great," he said, smiling without looking up from my file as he noted it.

At the end of our appointment, we got up.

"Thank you, doctor," I said, shaking his hand.

"You are welcome," he said, taking my hand and patting my shoulder with the other. "Good luck. I'll see you after your procedure."

Upon my return, I researched it. The internet spat out hundreds of links. I could not understand most of it. However, I felt relieved when it said it was an outpatient surgery involving precisely guided laser beams. From what I gathered, to sum it up, it said:

> *Stereotaxic surgery, or stereotactic procedure, is a minimally invasive neurosurgical technique that uses specialized equipment and imaging to precisely locate and treat abnormalities in the brain, breast, lung, or liver.*

I called UCLA and made an appointment. I was initially nervous, but it was quickly replaced with eager anticipation. I had a goal now.

When I was an inpatient at Long Beach Memorial and wheelchair-bound, I would constantly ask one question to any therapist that worked on me.

"Will I be able to stand up and walk?"

"We will see."

Needless to say, that wasn't the answer I was looking for. However, looking back, I realize they didn't want to give me false hopes. They were trying their level best to improve my condition. It's an uphill task that requires a specific type of skill. Also, they have to deal with various kinds of cases with different degrees of severity. It all can be overwhelming. I don't think I can ever do what they do. Kudos to them. Theirs is one of the many thankless jobs.

My procedure (I preferred that word over the ominous-sounding 'surgery') was two weeks away. However, I was told there wouldn't be a procedure that day. I was to see the doctors there, who would examine me and then give me an appointment for my procedure.

On the day of my first appointment, I drove up north on the 405 freeway for an hour. When I reached UCLA Medical Center, a pleasant receptionist directed me to the proper department. Soon, the doctor saw me. He studied my reports and the MRI scans I had done at Long Beach Memorial. He then made me perform some physical tasks to determine the state of my condition. He held out his arms and stretched his palms so the fingers were wide apart.

"Touch your nose and then touch my index finger," he said.

He then fisted his wrist and jutted out his index finger

"Focus your eyes on it."

I looked at it as he slowly moved it—up and down, left to right, all the while closely observing how my eyes moved.

"Good," he said, nodding. "Stand up and sit down."

I obeyed him. After making me do a few more tasks, he declared that I was qualified for the procedure.

I made my next appointment. On our way back, I was cheerful, and the notorious traffic on the 405 didn't dampen my spirits.

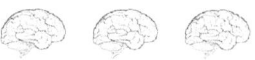

The doctors at UCLA Medical Hospital had advised me to come early in the morning. They needed enough time to prepare for the multi-phased surgery. I was not too sure about the procedure. I had many unanswered questions. What did the procedure entail? What would they be doing to me? Would I be put under? How long would the procedure last? My mind was flooded with many questions. Hence, to put me at ease, they patiently answered all my questions.

"How does it work?"

One of the doctors handed me a pamphlet. "Here."

"I will, but why don't you summarize it?"

He explained the process to me. As he proceeded, my eyes widened in amazement. It was quite an involved, multi-step process.

From what I gathered, it could be broken down into four steps.

Step 1: Attach a rigid frame to my skull. Dear reader, the best way to describe this gadget is for you to imagine a birdcage without any bottom and for steel rods instead of thin, vertical bars. And a tiny hole at the base with threadings. I would insert my head through the opening at the bottom. They then would screw it to a bed so that I would not be able to move my head while the laser beams pinpointed its target.

Step 2: I will have a CT Angio, in which a special dye is injected into my arm. It then travels through my veins to my brain, and pictures are taken of the vessels in the brain.

Step 3: They would study the pictures to determine the angle of the beam.

Step 4: Do the actual procedure.

On the day of the procedure, I got up at four a.m. and (along with my wife) drove to the medical center.

Thankfully, my in-laws were with us at home. They would be taking care of my children.

Since we left early—around five a.m., the traffic on 405 was thin. We made it to our destination in record time.

We parked our minivan in the underground parking. Since it was a long walk to the main lobby, my wife brought an empty wheelchair to the entrance.

"I'm sorry, but you *have* to use it. I know you don't like it, but the reception desk is far away. It'll be very hard for you to walk that distance. I know you've worked very hard to avoid getting into one. I wouldn't be asking you if I thought it was possible for you."

I looked at it with mixed feelings. While it was a lifesavior, it also was a constant reminder that I wasn't normal. I reluctantly sat in it. The dark memories of my prolonged stay returned.

After checking in, I took the elevator to where I was instructed to go. After changing into hospital clothes—which was unpleasant as it triggered the memory of a nightmarish past—I was asked to lie down on a hospital bed (again, not a pleasant experience). After a few minutes, a friendly doctor entered my room and greeted me with a big smile.

"Hi, I'll be fitting the frame on your head."

"Okay," I said nervously.

"Don't be scared. It's a straightforward procedure. You will be under general anesthesia. You won't feel a thing."

However, his reassurance had the opposite effect on me. Instead of feeling at ease, I was more alarmed now.

The doctors had advised me to avoid any solid food for twelve hours. I was wondering why, and now I had my answer. It didn't sound good. I had a flashback of my USC experience and shuddered. I looked in panic at my wife. I had read the material they had given me; nowhere did it say I would be put under it. Had I missed something?

Anesthesia?! Why does he have to put me under? I thought I would be awake when fitted. Isn't it a simple procedure of applying some sort of medical adhesive to my forehead and sticking the frame?

I sat up in my bed to ask him if it was possible to administer anesthesia locally. Also, general anesthesia is more dangerous than local anesthesia. How long would the procedure last? How long would I be under? I started to have doubts about my decision to have this procedure done. However, it was way too late to change my mind.

I had many questions. But before I could ask any questions, I was wheeled to an OR. I was shivering with fear. They misunderstood me as being cold and covered me with an extra sheet.

"Are you comfortable?" the nurse asked.

"Yes," I said.

I surrendered to my fate, closed my eyes, and inhaled the anesthetic.

When I opened my eyes next time, I was back in my room. It was as if I had magically teleported from the cold bed to a comfortable one. My eyelids felt heavy. I blinked. Slowly, a blurry face came into focus. I saw the doctor's smiling face.

"There you are," he exclaimed. "Hi."

"H—hi," I said groggily. I moved my head to find my wife, but I couldn't. My head felt heavy, as if it was balancing a load of bricks on top. Two rods—one on each side—obscured my peripheral vision. I felt as if I was behind bars in jail. My head was tightly welded to the frame. I tried to sit up in my bed.

"No, no," the doctor gently pushed me back. "Lie down. Don't try to move your head. How do you feel?"

"W—what happened?"

"Nothing, the procedure was successful. Here." He thrust a mirror in front of my face. Upon seeing my face, my jaw dropped. I felt as if I was punched in my gut. I was in disbelief. I took a deep breath. I looked at my face where the device was attached.

They had not used an adhesive to attach the frame. Instead, they had used medical screws to attach it to my skull. They must have used a drill to puncture my skin. An orange-colored liquid trailed from the attached screws.

Subconsciously, I moved my hand to feel it with my fingers.

"What's that?"

"Antiseptic," the doctor replied. "It'll dry up in an hour. Does it hurt?"

I shook my head. "No."

"Any headache?"

I shook my head again. "Nope."

He produced a tiny flashlight, switched it on, and aimed the shiny beam at my eyes, alternating from one to the other.

"Good," he observed. He turned it off, placed it back in his coat pocket, and proceeded to perform some basic tests to assess my agility.

Just then, a nurse appeared holding a Polaroid camera in her hand. "Look up," she said.

I looked at her, and, without any warning, I was briefly blinded by its flashlight. As the room reappeared, I looked at the doctor in annoyance.

"It's for our records," he explained as he fanned the photo to dry. He then handed it to me. "See."

My face gradually materialized. My caged and surprised face appeared.

My wife leaned forward to look. She gave me a meek smile.

I wished I could read her mind. *I must appear ridiculous to her.* I looked at her and smiled.

"How do I look?" I joked. "Do you think I can model for them?"

She looked at me and rolled her eyes. The look of relief on her face told me everything I wanted to know.

"Step one done," I said. "Three more to go."

"Very well. I'll let you rest." The doctor turned around to leave the room. "Call me if you feel any discomfort."

"Sure, thank you," I said. "By the way, how long will I have to wait in this?" I waved my hand over my face.

"Can't tell you the exact time, but it'll be long."

"Oh," I said. "Are there any restrictions?"

"Such as?"

"Food."

"Not at all," he said, smiling. "You can eat anything you want. The only thing you can't have is a diet drink after your CT Angio."

I was not much of a soda drinker, but I thirsted for one at that moment.

"Oh, but I can have a non-diet drink, right?" I asked.

He nodded. "Right." He looked at his wristwatch. "Do you have any other questions for me?"

"No," I said, shaking my head.

"Okey-dokey," he said, smiling as he left the room.

I looked at my wife.

"I'm going to the cafeteria soon," she said. "Do you need anything?"

"A chocolate bar."

"You and your chocolate," she said, smiling as she shook her head.

After a few minutes, she left.

I was all alone. I looked around my room. It was very similar to my one at Long Beach Memorial; it was clean, sterile, and devoid of emotions. Now, all I had to do was wait.

You have no choice but to go ahead with the rest of the procedure. Next, step two.

I closed my eyes and soon was asleep.

After being fitted with the frame, I was taken for a CT Angio. This, too, was a relatively painless procedure. Thankfully, I didn't have to be sedated during this procedure. They inserted a syringe in my arm that connected to a special dye. It was an automated procedure to deliver the payload. As the dye entered my body, I felt the warm liquid traversing through my veins and up my brain. It wasn't a pleasant feeling, but nothing close to the one I had during my MRI procedure.

The procedure ended very soon. I was pleasantly surprised at how short it had lasted. I had assumed that it would last, at least, as long as—if not longer—the MRI.

The adjacent door opened, and the technician walked out. He gave me a thumbs-up. "Very good, Mr. Aithal. We are done. The images are perfect."

"That's it?"

"Yup, that's it. I'll get your wife," he said as he pulled out the syringe from my arm.

"Thank you."

When she entered the room, she, too, looked surprised. Gingerly, I got up.

"Did the doctor tell you to avoid diet drinks?" the technician asked.

"Yes," I said, nodding.

"Good."

"Now?" I asked.

He looked confused. "What do you mean?"

"What do I have to do next?"

"Oh, now you wait."

"For?"

"The doctors will study the images to determine the laser beam's angle and intensity."

"Oh, I see." I nodded again as though I understood. However, I had absolutely no clue how they would analyze the images to determine the right angle and intensity.

"Do you know how long that will take?" I wondered aloud.

He shrugged. "A few hours."

"A few hours?!" I was surprised as I had not realized that step three would take so long. "What do I do?"

"You wait."

"Where do I go?"

Obviously, I was in no condition to go anywhere outside the building with a cage on my head.

"Go to the cafeteria, the gift shop, explore the hospital. It's a huge building. Just keep an eye on the time. Come back here after a few hours. We'll tell you where to go."

I groaned. "Oh." I had falsely assumed that the entire process would take less than half a day.

They had left a tiny part out: time. I had not realized the entire procedure would last the whole day. I would sit with the uncomfortable frame tied to my skull from sunrise to sunset. Although the frame is made of a light material, it feels heavy by the end of the day.

"Don't worry. They have done it many times."

The technician must have seen my hesitant expression. He, too, must have seen this confused look many times.

Steps one and two were performed in the morning. However, step three would take a very long time, and understandably so. Step four was going to be highly precise and irrevocable. Once done, they would not be able to reverse it. A tiny fraction off could have a devastating effect on me. There was no redo. I would be living with it for the rest of my life.

The area—the pons region—is a very tiny, narrow, and delicate area at the stem of the brain, with a jumble of thin veins concentrated in a small area. Even during my embolization procedure, the doctor didn't want to take any chances. He had to pull out the probe at the last minute, unsuccessfully. However, there was a vast difference between the two. Embolization was a revocable process, and this wasn't.

I tried to divert my mind by reading, talking—about nothing in particular—to my wife, watching TV, etc., constantly looking at the watch, hoping more time had passed. Further, to add to my misery, I could not go out until the procedure was complete. Hence, I was confined to four walls. Fortunately, I didn't have to lie down on a bed. I could sit in my wheelchair, and my wife and I explored the innards of the hospital: the cafeteria, the reception area, the gift shop, the maternity ward, the oncology department, etc. She also took me to a large window at the end of the hallway from where I could see the outside life: pedestrians, cars, traffic lights, tall buildings, a plane flying by in the sunny blue sky, etc.

I kept looking at my wristwatch. The time progressed at a snail's pace. The morning turned into an afternoon and then an evening. The streetlights came on, the traffic thinned, and fewer pedestrians occupied the sidewalks. The hustle-bustle subsided.

We went back to the CT Angio area.

Finally, they called me.

It was time for Step four. I was wheeled to a procedure room and made to lie down on a cold steel bed. They tightly screwed the frame to the bed so that my head would not move a millimeter during the process. After all, it was a very delicate procedure. Accuracy was of paramount importance.

A millimeter off the intended target could have dangerous and unknown consequences.

The brain is a mysterious organ. Although we have made much progress in understanding it, we have only scratched the surface. There are so many unknowns. We wrap our heads around it to make sense by creating neuron-firing graphics. However, the brain is much more complex than it is.

> Dear reader, as a layman, I've looked at the images of my brain to make sense. However, I confess I can't make heads or tails of it. For all you know, I could be staring at an image of a non-human brain.
>
> The only clue that I was looking at an image of my brain was from my name's sticker on the top-right of it.

To my surprise, step four lasted only for a few minutes. I felt nothing apart from a buzzing sound for a few seconds. Before I knew it had begun, it was over. I felt my head being unscrewed from the bed, lifted gently, and shifted to my wheelchair.

Although I had mentally prepared myself for a long climax, I was just relieved that the procedure was over.

"That's it?" I asked the doctor.

"That's it," he replied as he unscrewed the frame.

When he lifted the frame, I felt a heavy burden being lifted.

"How do you feel?" He looked at me.

I moved my neck up and down, sideways, and rotated it.

"Fine," I said, as my hand subconsciously moved to feel the holes. "How long would they last?"

"Oh, these?" he looked at them. "For about a week?"

"Hmm."

"Why? Do you feel any pain? Any discomfort?"

I shook my head.

"I can prescribe some painkillers," he said as he took out his prescription pad from his coat pocket.

"Nah." I shook my head again. "I'll be fine."

Also, and I didn't tell him, I have always avoided the pills.

I would prefer simply walking out of the hospital.

With two holes in my head.

We exited the now deserted parking lot. Soon, the minivan was speeding southbound on 405.

"How do you feel?" my wife asked.

"The same," I replied as I subconsciously massaged the back of my neck. I slowly moved my hand to my temple to feel the holes. It felt tiny and crusty to my fingers.

I was not feeling any difference in my condition.

I didn't realize then—what I do now—that the entire procedure was designed as a preventative measure, not a cure.

"Not even a tiny bit?"

I could see the disappointment on her face. However, I didn't want to give her any false hope.

"Not really," I replied. "But it may be too early to see any discernible difference."

"Okay," she said, yawning as we exited the freeway.

It was a long and tiring day for both of us. When we reached home, my in-laws were eagerly waiting to know how the day went. We briefly talked about it during our dinner and headed up to our bedroom.

Yes, *up*. By now, I had started going up to my bedroom. It may be very trivial for an average person, but it was an achievement for me. I would consider all these tiny things as a victory. It was exhilarating to sleep in my very own bed. As soon as my head hit the pillow, I was fast asleep.

The following morning, I made an appointment at UCLA for a follow-up visit. Soon, I returned to my daily therapy regimen.

I also called Dr. Adams to give him the progress report.

"I'll also be getting a copy of your results," he said. "Hang in there. I'm pleased with your progress. Keep doing what you are doing. When is your next appointment?"

"Next week."

"Keep me informed," he said.

Little did I realize how long I had to wait for the process to show any results.

> Dear reader, come to think of it, he must have known how the procedure worked.

The following week, I went back for a follow-up visit. I was keen to know whether the procedure had been successful. My wife and I were ushered into the doctor's office. Yes, it was an office, unlike an examination room. I was relieved to know that I would not have to change into a clownish hospital gown that would expose my backside.

The doctor was an African-American man in his mid-thirties. He wore round glasses that made him appear older. An expensive suit and a silk tie peeked underneath his doctor's coat. If he removed the white jacket, he could be a lawyer, a CEO, or any other executive sitting behind a desk. A stack of thick, yellow files lay on his rich mahogany desk. A few family photos were framed on his desk. One showed him beaming proudly at the camera, holding a big fish on a boat.

Behind him was a large shelf full of various medical books. To his right was a large window that overlooked the parking lot below. The gray carpet covered the floor. Soft jazz played in the background at a very low volume.

In one corner, a large screen displayed black-and-white images of my brain scan. The screen was divided into four quadrants, each showing different angles of my brain. He used his mouse to zoom in and out of a particular region of an image.

As we entered, he looked up and got up from his green leathered chair to greet us. "Come in, Mr. Aithal. Have a seat."

He waved his hand to the two empty chairs before the desk. He pressed a button on the remote control lying on his desk to turn off the music. We sat down and waited for him to speak.

"Lovely family," my wife commented, looking at the pictures.

"Oh, Thank you," he said, smiling proudly before looking back at the screen.

"Hmm," he continued, studying the images before him. My eyes silently oscillated between the screen and his face. He clicked his mouse to zoom into the image and leaned forward to study it closely. The occasional click of the mouse punctured the silence, the rhythmic tick of the clock on the wall, and a sporadic creak of the chair as he shifted to get a closer look. The suspense was killing me.

"Well?" I asked him eagerly.

"Huh?" His eyebrows furrowed as he looked at me in confusion. "Well, what?"

"What do you think? Did it work or not?"

His expression changed from a confused look to someone who now understood what I meant to a severe expression of a professor.

He leaned back in his chair. "Do you know how this process works?"

"Yes," I said, nodding. "I was there," I made a feeble attempt to crack a joke. I had read up on the process before I went in. However, I realized I had not read the whole article in my eagerness to improve. Now, I wish that I had read the material thoroughly.

"Well," he sighed. "Of course, you were there."

He interlaced his hands—as if praying, extended two of his index fingers on his lips, and looked at me thoughtfully as though it was not a laughing matter.

"Sorry," I said. "I didn't mean to make light of the matter."

"No worries," he said. "However, that was just part of the process."

"W—what? What do you mean?"

I was alarmed now. *Do I have to go through it again?*

"Please don't tell me I have to go through it again," I moaned.

"No, no," he said, shaking his head. "Nothing drastic like that. You are done with the cage. You won't have to go through it again."

"Then?"

"Now we have to wait and see if the process has worked. We will then examine your brain again and compare the two images."

"H—huh?" I was dumbstruck. My head was reeling from his words. I had to go through the CT angio again. Although it is a relatively painless process, I was not looking forward to it once again after a few weeks.

I expressed my displeasure. "Not again."

"I hear you," he said, in a sympathetic voice, "but we have to do it. That is the only way for us to know if it worked, okay?"

I didn't reply. I looked at my wife and raised my eyebrows. She nodded. Reluctantly, I nodded.

"Fine, let's do it. Let's get over with it."

"Great. I'll make an appointment for the procedure."

"P—procedure?" My heart sank. "You mean it's not just a CT Angio?"

"No," he said, shaking his head.

"Then how does it work? There's more?"

He nodded. "Yes, I'm afraid so."

"What do I have to do?"

"First, you will be given a mild sedative to relax you."

"A sedative?" I was alarmed. "Anesthesia? Will I be put under?"

"No," he said, shaking his head. "You will be administered it orally to relax you. You won't pass out, just drowsy."

"Okay,." I leaned forward. "Then?"

"Then we go up your vein, with a miniature camera, through the groin region."

"Oh," I exclaimed. "It's like embolization."

"Kinda. As I already told you, you won't be put under. And we won't be doing anything to the affected region. All we will be doing is taking a look at it on a big screen."

He fell silent while I processed the information. Although I was not looking forward to it, I had little choice. After all, having gone through the first half of the process, I wanted to know its final result.

"Now, can we make the appointment?" he finally said, breaking the silence.

I reluctantly nodded. "I—I guess."

"Great," he looked at the screen. "Let's see now. How about May?"

"May?" I was surprised. *He's looking at the wrong year.* "We are in June."

"That's right, but you see," the scholarly tone again. "We have to wait for a year."

"*What?*" I shouted, looking at him in disbelief. "A year? That long?"

"That's right," he said, nodding. "It takes about a year for us to see any results."

I groaned. "Man?"

A year was way too long. I looked dejectedly at my wife. She squeezed my palms. "It's okay."

"It's not as if you'll be stopping all your daily activities," the doctor said. "Immerse yourself in them, and soon you'll forget about the appointment.

"I guess."

"So, is June fine?" he said as he looked at his screen.

"Yes?" I said.

She nodded.

"Yes," I confirmed. "Do I need to do anything to prepare myself before the appointment?"

"No," he said, shaking his head. "Just be here as you are right now. I've booked you for an early morning procedure. You'll be the first patient."

"Great," I said as I got up from the chair. "That'll help me beat the traffic."

"That's right," he said, smiling as he looked at my file. "Cypress? Never heard of it. Where's that?"

"Orange County—north Orange County."

"Wow!" he exclaimed. "That's quite a drive."

"Yes." *But we'll be here on time.*

As we exited the hospital's parking lot, I told my wife: "I'm hungry."

"What do you feel like?" she asked, knowing what I'd say.

There was this cute little Mediterranean cafe that served excellent falafel sandwiches. Moreover, since it was far from where we lived, we would only go there when we were in the area.

"Let's go to the falafel place," I said.

"Sounds good."

We spent the next hour enjoying delicious hot falafel sandwiches and a cold beverage while discussing our next plan of action.

"What do we do next?" I asked, taking a big bite of my sandwich and washing it with the chilled soda.

"Nothing," she said, shaking her head casually.

"Nothing?!"

I was surprised. I stopped chewing my food and looked at her. "What do you mean, nothing?"

"We just keep doing what we are doing. We attend therapy sessions, go to the gym, meet our doctors regularly, etc. Apart from all these activities, we continue to socialize with our friends, go to parties, go for a drive, go out to restaurants, and so on. We will lead a regular life and soon forget about this."

I grunted. "Hmm." She was right. There was no point thinking about it every day.

As we were driving back, the ominous thought of the procedure was pushed back in my mind.

Upon reaching our house, I called Dr. Adams to give him an update. However, from the tone of his voice, I had a strange feeling he already knew the time it would take to see any results.

I reread the pamphlet. There it was in black and white. It said it took around a year to determine if the procedure had worked.

The doctor (and my wife) was right. Soon, I forgot about the appointment as I busied myself in my daily routine, only to be reminded of my appointment when someone asked me about the procedure.

Chapter 6

ONE YEAR HAD PASSED, DURING which time I didn't notice any change in my condition. I continued to go about my life, doing regular things: get-togethers, parties, going to the movies, going for long drives, etc.

I also continued my routine visits to the doctors and my therapy sessions. I was glad I could lead a regular life (well, as normal as possible). I had come to terms with my limitations. I knew I could not do several things I loved: trekking, biking, playing cricket (my favorite sport), golfing, etc. I had made a mental shift from having a negative mind to a positive thought. Instead of thinking about what I *couldn't* do, I began to think about what I *could.* Life had dealt me the worst hand. I had to turn it into a winning one. This mere shift in my thinking helped me tremendously.

> Dear reader, At the risk of sounding like a motivational coach, I highly recommend you try it too. You will be able to turn any dire situation in your favor. I am not talking about a physical

> hindrance but a mental one. I knew that, thankfully, my mental faculties were intact. I have used it to my advantage.

As the day of the appointment neared, I looked forward to it instead of dreading it. I had to know the results. After all, knowledge is power.

Some of my doctor-friends had warned me how delicate the procedure could be. Although it was non-invasive, it still entailed puncturing my body, inserting a thin rod, and going up to my brain. There were so many things that could go wrong—Murphy's Law- *anything that can go wrong will go wrong.* A tiny little misstep could mean curtains for me. I would not be the same person anymore.

One of my biggest worries was about my cognitive skills and memory. One of the things I had been fortunate about was my mental faculties. After seeing many people struggling with memory, I considered myself lucky. Many of them had their physical ability intact but could not communicate well. When I saw such people, I was always envious of them being able to walk normally. However, the moment they started conversing, it was obvious that they were struggling to hold a trail of thought.

> Dear reader, if you were in my (or their) shoes and had to choose one, what would it be? Your physical faculties or your mental acumen? It's tough to choose one over the other, right?

Finally, it was the day of my procedure. I drove to the UCLA Medical Center early in the morning with my wife. After checking in, I was directed to the prep room. I changed into the hospital gown and patiently waited in the room. Although I was looking forward to it, the moment had arrived, and I was a little nervous. I looked at my wife, seeking reassurance. I thought of my children. *What if something goes wrong? Will I be able to recognize them?*

After a while, a beautiful lady walked in. She had blond hair, a sparkling smile, and twinkling blue eyes. She was in her blue scrubs.

"Hello," she chirped.

"Hi," I greeted her back, clumsily. I was mesmerized by her beauty. For a moment, I forgot that I was wearing a clownish-looking hospital gown.

Wow, UCLA has some very pretty nurses. I extended my arm in her direction.

She looked confused. "Huh?"

"Aren't you here to take my vitals?"

She laughed. "Oh, no. I'm not a nurse. I'm the doctor who will perform the procedure on you today."

My jaw dropped.

Her smile told me that it happened to her all the time.

"We will be taking you to the OR in a short while. Do you have any questions for me?"

I shook my head sheepishly, avoiding her gaze.

"Great," she said, smiling as she got up. "All right then. See you soon."

Or not, I thought to myself as I realized that I would be mildly sedated. The next time I'd see her would be after the procedure.

I waved awkwardly. "Okay."

"Bye?"

My wife smiled at me as though reading my thoughts. I gave her a sheepish look.

Momentarily, the male nurse entered the room.

"Hi," he said, with a smile. "I'm here to take you to the OR."

"Right."

"But before we do that, I need to take your vitals," he said as he approached me. "Open your mouth, please."

I obeyed him, and he thrust a thermometer into my mouth. While it did its work, he checked my pulse. After a few seconds, he took it out of my mouth and noted the reading.

"Good. Normal," he muttered as he proceeded to take my blood pressure. Once he was satisfied that everything was normal, he reached into his pocket and produced a foil saying Xanax. He opened it and handed it to me with a cup of water.

"It'll help you relax," he explained.

I was surprised. "That's it? That's all I have to take?"

"Oh, no," he said, shaking his head. "You will be administered a stronger sedative in the OR."

He looked at my worried expression. "Don't worry. It's not an anesthetic. It's more meant to numb you. You'll be half-asleep during the entire procedure."

Soon, I was wheeled into the OR.

The nursing staff prepped me.

"Are you comfortable?" one of them asked me.

I nodded.

"Do you want some music?"

Music!? I shook my head. *What's with the music?*

"Okay then," she said as she proceeded to inject me with the sedative. Soon, as it traversed my veins, I began to feel its effect. I started to feel drowsy. I wasn't fully passed out, so I could see and hear what was happening around me: metallic objects clinking, beeps of monitors, hushed conversations, a hand gently touching my forehead as a masked face appeared in my blurry vision, etc.

Soon, a male doctor and a couple of assistants accompanied the pretty doctor. All I could see were their eyes as their faces were covered with masks.

"Are you okay? Can you hear me?" he asked.

Since I had already been administered a mild sedative by then, I was drowsy. I nodded slowly.

He nodded to the lady doctor. "He's ready."

The procedure started. I could feel faint thuds of instruments and clanks of objects.

Finally, I felt a tiny prick next to my groin region, followed by a cold object being inserted. Since the area was already numbed, I didn't feel any pain—just the sense of touch.

The pretty doctor's masked face appeared in front of me. "Are you okay?"

I merely nodded. As the tiny wire made its way through my vein, I could see the video as it made its way to my brain. I felt as if I was seeing a silent documentary of an object making its way through a narrow tunnel. It would momentarily stop and adjust itself when the doctor gently twisted it to overcome an obstacle and plod further to its destination.

Suddenly, it stopped. It had reached its destination. It was surreal to see a live feed of my brain.

> Dear reader, Have you heard about Alice in Wonderland Syndrome? It's a brain condition that disrupts the brain's ability to process sensory input. It affects how one perceives the size of things around them and the feel or look of one's body. It can also distort one's sense of reality.
>
> I felt as if I was Alice in Wonderland. The screen seemed to change its state from a solid to liquid. I was falling into a dark, bottomless abyss. The doctors were caricatures of themselves—a cardboard cutout. I could be in Dali's surrealistic painting.

The feeling was jarring. I didn't know how long the procedure would last. After a while, I closed my eyes and fell asleep.

When I woke up, I was back in my room. I felt a dull pain with a throbbing sensation on the right side of my groin. I looked down. A giant bandage covered the area where they had inserted the probe.

Subconsciously, I moved my hand to feel it.

A nurse stopped me. "No. No. Leave it alone for a while. The less you touch it, the faster you'll heal."

"When can I remove the bandage?"

"In a few days."

"Can I shower with it on?"

"Of course," she said, nodding. "Just make sure to dry it well." She handed me a tube. "After removing it, apply this ointment in the region."

Just then, the doctor came to check on me. Now, she wore a white coat over her scrubs and had a stethoscope around her neck.

"There is my patient," she said, smiling. "How do you feel?"

I nodded meekly. "Okay." I winced a little when I motioned to sit straight.

"No, no," she said, shaking her head. "Stay lying down. You still are recovering."

She shoved her hand in her pocket and took out a prescription pad.

"I'm prescribing some painkillers." She wrote something on it. "Take it with food," she said as she tore off the paper from her pad.

"Sure, doctor," I said. "Is there anything else I need to know?"

She shook her head as she got up. "No," she said, patting my shoulders. "That's it."

I was ready to go home.

Now, all I had to do was wait for my results. Fortunately, the wait wasn't long. After a few days, I returned to find them out. I felt like a nervous college boy waiting to find out whether he had passed or failed. However, this was different. Soon, I would know if the procedure had worked and if the year-long wait would be worth it.

I was keen on knowing the outcome. One year had passed since my surgery, and I had not noticed any difference. Of course, I didn't expect to be cured entirely and start running. However, I was hoping that I'd see improvement in my condition. However, as I previously stated, the procedure was designed to be a preventive measure, not a cure.

Upon reaching the medical center, I was ushered into the same familiar office I had been in over a year ago. The same doctor greeted me warmly and asked me to take a seat. The screen in front of him displayed the familiar images of my brain scan. I noticed two sets of my scans, one from one year ago and the other from a few days ago. His eyes moved from one set to another as he compared the two images. Now and then, he would use his mouse to zoom in and lean forward to get a closer look. After a few minutes of silence, I couldn't bear the suspense any longer.

"Well?" I looked at him eagerly. "What do you see? Did it work?"

He leaned back in his chair and looked at me. "Yes," he replied, "But."

"But?"

I was alarmed. *I don't want any buts. Buts are never good, and the sentence following after a but is never good.*

I looked at my wife. Blood had drained from her face. She, too, looked worried.

"But, what, doctor?" she asked.

"During the scan, we discovered two more aneurysms," he replied in a grave tone.

"W—what?"

My jaw dropped. I was shocked. I stayed silent for a while, too stunned to speak. For a few seconds, my brain ceased to think. I felt a dark cloud gather over it.

The doctor saw my gloomy expression. "Did you hear what I said?"

"Yes," I said, nodding as I snapped out of the stupor, and my brain started functioning again. This didn't sound very good. Enduring the trauma once was enough for me. My body was a few years older now. I don't know if it could withstand one more blow—physically and mentally. *Oh no, Not again!*

"How did it happen? Why wasn't it discovered in previous scans? Did they miss it?" I asked with a worried look.

"No, no," he said, shaking his head vigorously. "They didn't miss it."

"Then?

"It simply wasn't there before."

"Huh?" I was confused. "What do you mean 'it wasn't there?'"

"It wasn't there before your sur—, er, procedure, the Stereotactic Surgery," he explained.

I noticed that he, too, had used the word 'procedure' instead of 'surgery.'

"It was probably formed due to the heat of the laser. It's a widespread occurrence of its side effects."

"Oh."

"The good news is that it's very tiny and has formed in a different region."

How can two more aneurysms be good news, I thought.

"Where?"

"It's in the front of your face, running along your neck region," he said as he ran down his index finger down his neck.

He turned the screen to face me. "Look."

I leaned forward. I tilted it a little more to adjust the glare of the sunlight from the windows. I wasn't sure what to look for. I narrowed my eyes.

"What am I looking for?" my eyes darted between the images and his face.

He saw the confused look on my face.

"See these," he traversed his finger over the image. "They are newly formed. These weren't there one year ago."

"Oh," I said, feebly. I looked at the screen but couldn't understand what I was looking for. If he had not pointed them out, I wouldn't be able to find them. I simply nodded as if I had understood.

The doctor turned the screen back towards him. I leaned back in my chair. Many questions were swarming like a vortex in my mind. Apart from the hows, whens, and whats (which had already been answered), I wanted to know more.

"So, what do we do? What are my choices? And please don't tell me one more surgery," I said crestfallen.

"No, no. Nothing drastic like that."

"So," I said, narrowing my eyebrows, "we do nothing?"

"Not really. All we have to do is to monitor it regularly."

"That's it?"

"Well," he hesitated, "you know it involves you taking more scans, right?"

"Oh dear," I groaned. I had not anticipated it. "That means I must get in that narrow, closed tube again."

"Well…," he trailed off. "You have a choice. You know there are two types of MRI scans, right?"

"No," I said.

I was desperate to take any alternate measures to avoid the dreaded tube, and my curiosity was piqued. "Tell me more about them."

"You have the closed one that you have experienced in the past, or you can do an open MRI."

"Really?" my eyes brightened.

"Yes, really," he said as he opened his desk drawer to hand me a leaflet. "Here you go. Please go through it."

"Why wasn't I informed of this before? I would have chosen to do this instead of the closed MRI," I said, irritated. "I could have saved myself from going through the torture."

"I understand how you feel, but they are less reliable."

"What do you mean?"

"Sometimes, the results are not clear. In such cases, they need to retake the scans."

"Oh," I said. "What do you recommend?"

"Most of the doctors prefer the results from a closed MRI."

I looked disappointed.

"I realize that it's not something you wanted to hear," he quickly added, "but its results are more reliable. It's better to take a Xanax and power through it for forty minutes or so. I agree that they are not a pleasant experience. However, as you would know, they are way better than surgery—way safer."

"Hmm," I said, lost in my thoughts.

I was not looking forward to going into the claustrophobic tube, but I realized that it was my best choice.

"Also, it's better to do it only once rather than taking a chance of going through it multiple times," he said, to drive home the point.

"Fine," I said finally. "Let's do a closed one. Where do I go for it?"

"You are in Orange County, right?" he said as he looked up my address.

"Yes," I said, nodding. "Why?"

"You don't *have* to come here to do it. You can do it in your area and email me the results. If I see any changes in your condition, I'll call you."

"How often do I have to do it?"

"Every six months," he replied as he got up from his chair to indicate that the meeting was over.

We did the same.

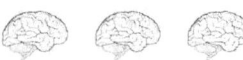

When we reached the parking lot, I asked my wife, "Feel like a falafel sandwich?"

"Sure," she replied, realizing that it would help me to take my mind away from what had transpired a few minutes ago.

We drove to the restaurant. After eating there, we ordered a few more to carry with us. Hopefully, I'd never have to return to the medical center again.

Thankfully, I was right. That was the last time I visited UCLA Medical Center.

Over the years, I've gone through this torture many times, and I am happy to say that the aneurysms have been the same. I have resigned to having to do this many times for the rest of my life. It doesn't bother me as severely anymore. I've mastered the routine. I take Xanax half an hour before my scan. It helps me relax. Since I have taken it, my wife has driven me to the scanning center. I do my thing. I meet my neurologist after a few days. He studies the images and informs me of the results. So far, there hasn't been a change. I guess I'll cross the bridge when I come to it. Meanwhile, instead of brooding over it, I go about my life as though nothing has happened.

Also, an open MRI is open from one end, but your head is still in the narrow tube. You can't avoid it. I think it's better to go through the closed one once and get it over with instead of taking a chance with an open one. If the scan results aren't satisfactory, you'll have to go through it again.

Besides, I have little choice in the matter. I have to *divert* my mind. Besides, and all those who know me will vouch for it, I'm a very positive person.

I look forward to the future instead of delving into the past.

After Stereotactic Surgery

As time progressed, the fateful day became a distant memory—like a nightmare I wanted to forget. However, I was reminded of that day every six months when I had to do my MRI scan. By now, even though I was used to the routine, I was always nervous as the day neared. And then, I would anxiously wait for my next appointment to see the doctor. Only when he cleared me would I relax again—until the next time. I guess I have resigned to this cycle. It has become a task I *must* complete every six months. It has now become part and parcel of my life.

I also was reminded how lucky I was whenever I saw someone who had suffered a stroke. I didn't know if the tragedy was recent, something that had occurred long ago, or how severe it was. From my past experience, I knew that there was nothing I could do but be empathetic—and not sympathetic. I would approach them and encourage them.

Once, while exercising at the gym, I saw a man with a walker. He was in his late forties or early fifties. His young son followed him from one piece of equipment to the other, assisting him in setting it up so that he could perform his exercises.

That made me think. His son appeared in his teens, probably a high school kid. Even though he would be more than happy to do so, accompanying his father would eat into his time. Besides, he would have to do it once his school ended for the day. He would only be able to do it for a limited time. He, too, had his own life, homework, friends, etc. And what would the man do once he went off to college?

I approached them. "Hi," I said.

He looked up. His face frowned as if he didn't know me. His son stopped wiping down the equipment and looked up at me.

Who is this stranger? What does he want? he must have thought.

"Yes?" he narrowed his eyebrows, looking annoyed to be interrupted. I could relate to how he felt. He wanted to be left alone. He wanted to finish his routine and get out as soon as possible.

"Can I help you?" his son asked, looking at his wristwatch. Probably, he had to attend to other things. I smiled at both of them.

"I just wanted you to know you are doing a great job," I told the father. "Take it from me: Things get better. Look at me. I, too, suffered from a stroke a while ago."

Instantly, his expression changed to a smile. He looked me up and down.

"Thank you."

"Keep it up. Never give up—never."

All he needed was a little encouragement from a stranger who had been through it. Like me, he was not looking for sympathy, just kind words.

"You, too, are doing a great job," I told his son.

"Thank you," he said, smiling.

We spent another few minutes discussing our conditions. The father wanted to talk more, but I realized it would be unfair to his son.

"I'll let you get back to your exercise," I told him, noticing his son looking at his wristwatch. He looked relieved that the conversation had ended.

Also, I noticed a man standing, shooting daggers, waiting impatiently for the equipment to be free.

"Okay," he said, shaking my hand.

"I'll see you around," I said as I returned to my equipment.

Sure, he must have been encouraged, just like me. "You are doing great," "Awesome job," "Very nicely done," and so on. However, various therapists must have uttered all these encouraging words, which helps tremendously. However, when a stranger says these words in an environment outside of a medical establishment, they have a profound impact.

Since then, the man has always smiled whenever he sees me and approaches me. We shoot a breeze for a little while before returning to our routines.

Also, *Keep on trying. Never Give Up* has been my mantra. In fact, years ago, my article was published in a 'brain' magazine. It was titled, you guessed it, Keep Trying. Never Give Up.

I genuinely believe that in addition to a loving family and close friends, these kind words by strangers helped me immensely in my mental recovery. My family and friends know me; they know how I think. They are aware of all my idiosyncrasies—and tolerate them, but it makes a huge difference when it comes from someone who has already been through it before. Unlike most people, my words significantly impact them more as they know I'm one of them; I've already been through it.

When I was in the hospital, one of the doctors who visited me frequently was a psychologist. He was ensuring that my mental state was intact and that I was not going into depression. Many people who have suffered from a traumatic brain injury have gone through this debilitating condition. Once, he took the trouble of seeing me at the 'halfway house' after my discharge.

He smiled as he gazed at me under his glasses. "Do you mind if we spend some time talking about things?"

I was relieved that I would not be attending a therapy session. "Sure."

"Is there somewhere we can be alone?" he asked the therapist.

"We have a bedroom downstairs that is always empty. Will that do?"

"Perfect. Thank you."

He led me to the room. Calling it a bedroom was a bit of a stretch as there was no bed. Just a table and two chairs. He sat in one and asked me to do the same. I sat across from him, drumming my hands on the table, waiting for him to start the conversation. He opened his leather briefcase, took out a yellow notepad and a pen, closed it shut, and put it near his feet.

"Let's start," he said, smiling. "How do you feel?"

"Fine."

"It must be great to sleep in your own bed."

"Oh yes," I said.

"Do you sleep well at night?"

"Yes."

He tapped his pen on the notepad. He realized that it was a one-way conversation. He was not getting through to me, so he changed his tactic. To make me feel more comfortable, we talked for a few hours about various other topics, from sports to food. During that time, I had forgotten that I was the patient and he was the doctor. It was as if two men were casually talking. I had not realized it, but all the while, he was taking notes.

I didn't think much of it then, but now I realize how vital it was to check my mental well-being along with my physical improvements.

Also, in the early days in the hospital, when I was in no condition to speak to anyone, the other challenging task was dealing with the insurance company. Thankfully, my wife had my back. She not only dealt with them but also read up on each and every medication that was administered to me to know its side effects.

> Dear reader, As you know, many medicines have many side effects. To get rid of one symptom,

> they may introduce several others. If you have noticed, the commercials broadcast on television show the wonder drug that will cure your ailment. However, if you read the fine print (and sometimes they mention it at the end of it—at a breakneck pace), it lists a litany of side effects.

Whenever I visit my doctor now, I ask him about a drug by its name.

"Where did you hear about it?" he asks.

"On a TV commercial. It said to talk to your doctor, so I'm talking to you."

His reaction to this is always the same—a shake of the head, exasperated laugh, and such.

"These TV commercials have turned you into a monster. You ask about them without understanding their after-effects or if they will clash with the other medicines you are taking already. They never tell you that, do they? These commercials can do more harm than good to your body. I wish Congress did something about it."

He was right. These TV advertisements featuring happy people have caused headaches for doctors across America. Although they claim to provide knowledge and enrich lives, they do more harm than good.

> Dear reader, did you know that the United States and New Zealand are the only two countries in the world that allow direct-to-consumer (DTC) advertising of prescription drugs on television?

Watching them, I always smile and shake my head in disgust. They show happy people going about their lives, at a restaurant with their friends, playing with their children or grandchildren, etc. They never show what can go wrong. They always end by saying, 'Talk to your doctor.' In my opinion, these commercials have created more headaches for doctors.

The viewer will feel empowered by knowledge, but a little knowledge is a dangerous thing.

Google and YT

It has been a challenging journey but a rewarding one. When I've felt low, I've thought about things to look forward to, and diverting my mind has helped me lift my spirits. I've always kept my mind busy. Even when my body is resting, my mind is racing.

A very long time ago, when I was growing up in India, a friend once asked me what my favorite hobby was.

"Thinking," I had replied.

He had laughed. "Are you crazy? Do you think you are Einstein?"

It was all in jest then, but years from now, I realize how prominent it has become.

When I wake up every morning, I prepare a mental checklist of things I want to accomplish during the day, and at night, I take stock of the things I've been able to do. Every day is a fresh start to a bright future.

By nature, I've always been curious about mundane things. That keeps me going. For example, if I go to a restaurant and see a painting of village life, I imagine how it would be to live there. Crazy, right? But these little things have helped.

The internet has been my savior, especially Google and YouTube. I have used them extensively—not just to learn but to explore the world. The internet has been my window to the world. I've seen faraway places I'd never see otherwise: the peak of Mount Everest, the Arctic, the Amazon Jungle, etc. Honestly, even if I was fit, I don't think I'd see any of the places in person. However, it makes an enormous difference in thinking that *I could*, instead of *I can't*.

> Dear reader, isn't it true for almost all of us? When we are forbidden to do something, we want to do it more. It's in our nature.

I am a software developer. When I came to this country in 1989, I worked on IBM midrange machines. My other memoir, Confessions of an Indian Immigrant: Dawn of IT Opportunities in the Land of Promise, describes my journey from India to the U.S. when the Indian offshore business was in its infancy. In fact, I doubt if the word 'offshore' was associated with it. It was meant to describe other things: offshore drilling, offshore oil rigs, etc.

I worked as a programmer on the AS/400, a successor of S/38 (who was a successor of S/36). Some of the current crop of developers may not even have heard of it. They were the new shiny objects in their heydays, robust workhorses, highly in demand, dependable, etc. They were rarely visible on the front end but were famous as dependable business machines. However, over the years, their demand has decreased. The Internet has changed everything. Everything is browser-based, with colorful graphics and videos. AS/400s, with their text-based, green-screened UI, was no match for modern technologies.

> Dear reader, one of the only places I still have seen them being used on front desks is Costco. Whenever I see them there, it transports me back to my early days in this country.

After all, the only constant in our lives is change. Even though I get dozens of newsletters in my inbox daily about what's going on in the world of technology, I find it hard to keep up. There is so much information to process in so little time. And I've barely scratched the surface of the information deluge. This doesn't include sports, entertainment, politics, etc.

Also, it's an uphill battle to sort out information from misinformation in the currently charged political climate, which is becoming toxic day by day with the advent of AI-generated fake images. It's getting harder to decipher real news from fake.

To add to my woes, every time I took a vacation that lasted more than a week, I always felt the world had passed by upon my return, and I had lots of catching up to do. It's getting more challenging to keep on top of the information by the day.

However, having said that, I genuinely believe that my mind is less than half full of information with half of my life over. There still is plenty of room.

I've always maintained that we are in maintenance mode once we cross fifty. Let me clarify: Only our bodies should be in maintenance mode, not our minds.

These are merely my personal opinions. Please don't misunderstand it as a motivational speech. I'm not qualified to be one. My intention is to inspire others who are going through what I've gone through. I want them to know that the situation is not hopeless. There's a bright light at the end of a very dark, long, and lonely tunnel. To make them leave their comfort zone and venture into the unknown. All they have to do is take the first step towards it. Yes, it's easier said than done, but it is possible.

Things get better.

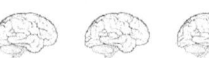

I had to reeducate myself in current technology or be labeled a 'has-been' who sees the world pass them by. I chose the former. Over the years, I've met many such 'have-been.' Fortunately, most have already retired and are living their golden days. However, I was not ready yet. I was too young and had many fruitful years ahead.

Before my stroke, I didn't know the inner workings of a browser or how to develop a website. I spent many hours watching training videos and learning. As I progressed, I started to appreciate the complexity of the web. Many moving parts are constantly happening behind the scenes before a simple webpage can be assembled and presented to the user.

To me, it has been a rewarding journey. It has helped my mind be constantly occupied with mastering new technology. As they say, one doesn't realize the passage of time when one's having fun. Over time, I have developed several websites for my family members and friends.

> Dear reader, you might think that writing is my passion. Well, you're mistaken—it's not. Computer is my passion. More broadly, technology is. In fact, I have enjoyed developing websites for my books more than writing them. Don't get me wrong. That doesn't mean I've not enjoyed writing it. All I'm saying is I've enjoyed developing the website more.

I've experienced the era of pagers, phone booths, cell phones (before they were smartphones), midranges, mainframes, spool tapes for backups, floppy disks, etc., and they have always impressed me. I love to embrace new technologies.

If there is one regret I have, it is that I won't be around to see new technologies being introduced a century later.

All I can do is to fantasize.

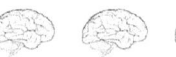

Also, some friends have faded over the years, but many have stuck by me. And I can understand, as it's a task to invite me. Before my stroke, I was the fun person, the life of the party. And now things are way different. Instead of having big parties, I prefer a smaller get-together with close friends. And they have been consistently mindful of my needs.

Once, somebody asked me what it felt like. That made me think. I've heard one word in every therapy session I've attended: coordination. Yes, that is a physical trait someone like me strives to be. However, *rhythm* is the word I prefer to describe me externally and internally.

A stroke disturbs the rhythm of life. Many tasks that an average person may take for granted get magnified. *How many steps are there to climb to go to a restaurant? How far are the restrooms? Did (s)he understand what I said? Did (s)he get the joke (I have a weird sense of humor)? Was my facial expression coordinating with what I was trying to convey?* These are just a few examples of thoughts that swirl around in my mind.

It may be my paranoia, but I can tell from the opposite person's response if they understand what I'm saying. I've learned to speak slowly and clearly and enunciate my words. I often find myself jumbling the words when I try to talk fast.

Also—and this is entirely my fault, I assume the opposite person knows what I'm talking about. I sometimes have this inner dialog and then continue my trail of thoughts loudly, only to see a confused look at the opposite person.

"Context, dad. Context," my daughter often tells me.

However, one thing that has been paramount to me has been my sense of humor. I genuinely believe that if you take life too seriously at every turn, it will overwhelm you. I always find a funnier side in a serious situation.

It reminds me of a lyric from a Hindi song:

जो तुम हसोगे तो, दुनिया हसेगी, रोओगे तुम तो ना रोएगी दुनिया.

(*jo tum hasoge to, duniya hasegi, rooge tum to na roegi duniya*) — loosely translated, if you laugh, the world laughs with you; if you cry, the world won't cry.

Samarpan

* * *

In 2007, my daughter had her *Samarpan* in *Kathak*[7]. Indians familiar with the *Arangetram*[8] in *Bharatnatyam*[9] can relate to it. A *Samarpan* is equivalent to an *Arangetram* of two disciples of classical Indian dance. It's not very common in *Kathak*. Although not alike, think of it as a quinceanera in a Latino culture or a bar/bat mitzvah in a Jewish culture. These are just a few examples I know. I'm sure each culture has its traditions that I am unaware of.

Even though I'm from India, it has many religions, and each has its own traditions, so there are many traditions I'm unaware of. In fact, after coming to this country, I have had the privilege of getting to know India more, as I've met various people from other parts of India. Growing up in Mumbai—Bombay, I only knew Mumbaikars. It didn't matter which part of India one was from. To me, they were all Mumbaikars. It truly is a melting pot.

Samarpan was a grand affair requiring a lot of planning and logistics—akin to a wedding. Invitations were designed

---

[7] Kathak is one of the nine major forms of Indian classical dance. Its origin is attributed to the traveling bards in ancient northern India known as Kathakar, who communicated stories from the Hindu epics through dance, songs and music. Source: Wikipedia

[8] An arangetram is a debut performance for a student of Indian classical dance and music, marking the end of their training and the start of their professional career. The word "arangetram" is a Sanskrit phrase that translates to "ascending the stage". It's a portmanteau of the Tamil word for stage ("arangu") and ascent ("etram"). Source: Wikipedia

[9] Bharatanatyam is an Indian classical dance form that originated in Tamil Nadu, India. It is a classical dance form recognized by the Sangeet Natak Akademi, and expresses South Indian religious themes and spiritual ideas of Hinduism and Jainism. Source: Wikipedia

and sent to the guests. A performance center was booked. The catering menu was finalized.

My daughter had spent countless hours rehearsing—perfecting her routine. Her teacher hired the musicians and the singers. We had booked a hall for her performance. A professional videographer was hired. My in-laws and sister-in-law flew in from India to attend the event, and my friends and my wife's cousin flew in from different states.

In fact, one of my close friends flew from New Jersey to surprise me. I didn't know about it. I was in the hall, enjoying my daughter's final dress rehearsal. My in-laws, too, were there. Suddenly, my wife approached me and told me I had to drive to the airport.

"Why?" I asked, showing my displeasure. "Who's coming?"

Everyone from different states who were attending the event had already arrived.

"Never mind who," she said, smiling mysteriously. "Just go with my dad."

He, too, was annoyed as he was enjoying my daughter's performance. The airport was far away from the hall, and going there would mean that he would miss the rest of the rehearsal.

"Can't we go after this is over?" he protested.

"No," my wife said, shaking her head. "She must have landed."

Hmm, 'she,' I thought. *Who could it be?*

Soon, the mystery was solved. As I drove near the terminal, I saw her standing at the curb. My jaw dropped. I couldn't believe my eyes. A silly grin spread across my face. It was my friend. Not even in a thousand years would I expect her.

I looked at my father-in-law and saw him smiling.

"No way," I guffawed. "You knew about this?"

"Yes," he said, and smiled. However, his mood changed when we returned to the hall. The rehearsal had ended, and he had missed a significant part of the dance.

"You shouldn't have made me go," he scolded my wife. "You very well know how much I enjoy Indian classical music, and my granddaughter is dancing to it, too. What more can a man want?"

My friends, too, participated in the event. By participating, I mean helping me with several tasks. In addition to booking a professional videographer, my friends also captured the moment on their own camera. Since we had not hired professional decorators, many of my friends helped us decorate the hall. At the end of the performance, many of us gave thank-you speeches. It was a memorable evening. One I still cherish now.

> Dear reader, you must wonder *why he is telling me all this and how it relates to this story*. I'll let you know why. Had I not been around, I would have missed this joyous occasion. This was a significant milestone in my life, in addition to attending my children's award ceremonies, attending my son's soccer games and swim lessons, and seeing them graduate.
>
> Also, there is more to life than therapies, gyms, exercises at home, doctor's visits, and MRI scans. I have gone through them so I can enjoy life. They have been an essential part of my journey but not my ultimate destination.

Just like this occasion, I've crossed many milestones in my life. I may briefly write about them to inspire those who think they have little to look forward to.

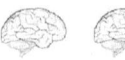

In 2013, my wife and I celebrated our 25th wedding anniversary. Once again, my in-laws flew in from India, and my wife's cousin (and her daughter), too, flew in from India. We had a party in my backyard. Once again, my friends decorated my backyard and set up the tables and chairs; my children performed for me, and so did my friends.

My wife's cousin, a chocolatier, handmade a special feast for the occasion. There was music and dancing. We played several games, and our guests participated enthusiastically. We had a photo booth to capture the moment. It was my day—my wife and I were the center of attention. I didn't want the evening to end.

As days passed, I had a bright idea. It would kill two birds with one stone. Hence, to preserve the memory, I have created a website. Occasionally, I visit it to take a walk down memory lane. Since website development was new to me then, it helped me learn a lot. This way, I could have a perfect solution serving two purposes. It would not only act as a time capsule for posterity but also help me learn.

Again, I am lucky to be alive and to have crossed this milestone. I have come a long way from that horrible day and have many to thank.

After all, it takes a village, there is no pleasure without pain, etc. Yes, these are all good sayings. However, to me, they *mean* something; they are not merely sayings.

Growing up in India, I attended karate classes. They were held thrice weekly, and each session lasted three hours. I did that for five years. It was very vigorous. At the end of each session, my *gi* would be soaking wet in my sweat. This strengthened my body, hardening it to withstand physical trauma. We sparred without any protective gear. Our *sensei*

also conducted a karate camp for a week on a hillstation. During that one week, all we would do was eat, sleep, and do karate.

Not only has it helped me tremendously in overcoming many physical disabilities, but it has also helped my body heal faster after the initial shock. Also, my body has learned to endure pain. Thanks to karate, I have a higher threshold to endure it. My *sensei* had this favorite phrase: *it's all mind over matter.*

This and other outdoor activities I have done in the past have rewarded me. In college, I went trekking for fifteen days in the Himalayas with my friends. We trekked on a circular route, going from one camp to another, sleeping in tents, having our meals near a campfire, and roughing it out.

Once again, I digress.

This is a memory I cherish; however, I think it's not part of this memoir. I am merely mentioning these moments to show how they have all rewarded me now.

I've learned over the years that no matter how mundane or boring an activity may be at the time you are doing it, do it. You don't have to enjoy it. Think of it as a future investment in your well-being. We all think of investing in our future in terms of money, but have you ever considered investing in your body? After all, what would you do with all the wealth you have collected if your body was not there to enjoy it? As the cliched saying goes, *health is wealth.*

For example, just before my daughter's *Samarpan*, we—my daughter and I—spent several hours on the computer to create an AV presentation for the event. I could do it quickly only because I had spent many hours in the past learning new technologies. It had never crossed my mind then that I'd put this knowledge to use in this manner.

There is a famous verse in Bhagavad Gita which says,

कर्म करो, फल की चिंता मत करो।

Karm karo, fal ki chinta mat karo' which means: Do your duty without thinking about results. In other words, when one considers what is within his power to do, he realizes that one can work hard towards a goal. Whether he will be successful or not is not in his hands. But when one puts in the effort, one is more likely to be successful.

My intention is not to lecture you. I'm saying this out of experience. I've been there, through tough times, and emerged on the other side of a long tunnel. Yes, it takes time, but what choice did I have? As I said earlier, fate had dealt me a losing hand. It was up to me to make it into a winner.

24 years

Wow! I can't believe it has been twenty-four years. Time flies. To say the least, it has been one helluva and a long train journey through life with many stops. Along the way, many have joined me on my adventure. Although some of them may not even be aware, several of them have had a lasting impact on my life. It would be presumptive of me to tell anyone what to do. I can merely narrate my story. How you want to tackle life's challenges is up to you.

As I reflect on my life now—in 2024, when I pour down my thoughts, I realize how far I've traveled in my journey of recovery. It has been twenty-four years since that fateful day when my life changed forever within a few seconds. Like any other difficult task, there have been good days and bad, ups and downs.

I'm not going to sugar-coat it. I'm not here to give you a rosy picture. Yes, it's a tough road ahead. There have been moments when I felt the situation was hopeless. There have been many challenges along the way, but the results have been rewarding.

Nobody can foretell the future, but each individual can determine how to make it brighter and more rewarding. The path you will choose to travel on will determine your destination.

Many have asked me how I feel about it after so many years. It's a tragedy that can't be predicted, nor can it be averted. One minute, you are perfectly fine, and the next second, you are not. However, I consider myself extremely lucky (hence the title) to have had a good life.

I've been fortunate to travel to India (among other countries) several times. I have seen my children grow from minors to successful adults, and I've attended their graduations.

I've been fortunate to be free to drive without being restricted to assisted devices attached to myself or the vehicles. To me, it has been the ultimate expression of freedom.

I've been able to go to restaurants and enjoyed trivial things in life that anyone else takes for granted. Sure, I am aware of my restrictions. However, I've concentrated on the positives instead of magnifying my shortcomings by giving them much thought. I've strived to lead a normal life—as normal as I can.

I'm not a motivational speaker. I'm merely expressing my experiences. I do understand that each case is different and unique. There are those who have suffered a stroke who are affected severely, and they have their own journey. I'm not disregarding this. However, as you can see, I've overcome many challenges. A friend once told me that what has stayed with me is that *what doesn't kill you will only make you stronger.*

> Dear reader, once again, at the risk of sounding preachy, let me tell you that the human body is

fantastic. It can do much more than you think it can handle. As my *sensei* always used to say, *it's just a question of mind over matter.* It can endure a lot of abuse when you are young. It has a unique ability to heal and correct itself. It just needs proper care and time.

Suppose you can hike Mount Everest at the age of seventy, great! Do it—more power to you. However, I believe the body requires more maintenance once you cross fifty. You may be young at heart, but not your body. Listen to your body. You have to be honest with yourself about your abilities.

Once again, as usual, I digress. Let's get back to what I've been able to do.

I've attended various parties, seen my friends' children grow up and get married, and had the great pleasure of seeing the next generation begin their life adventures.

As I've repeatedly said before, I've had the pleasure of pursuing something I really enjoy: long drives. I look forward to taking my friends and relatives to show them around.

I'm reminded of my shortcomings now and then, but they are at the back of my mind now. I've decided not to focus on them but to enjoy life.

My sense of humor and ability to take my situation lightly have kept me going. You can not take life too seriously, or it may overwhelm you. It's in your hands to mold your future. You must be careful to avoid pitfalls but can't be afraid to live.

And above all, I've never felt sorry for myself for my condition. People around me have helped me boost that. I've never seen a look of pity on their faces.

Although they are all in my mind, I've had innumerable personal victories. It's this mental game I play with myself.

I've set out to achieve a task and felt rewarded for successful completion, no matter how small it may be. I highly recommend trying it. It's exhilarating.

It has been a long and arduous journey. However, it has been a richly rewarding one.

Anyone who has suffered a stroke has a decision to make., a path to choose their future. Either you feel sorry for yourself, or you do something about it. I chose the latter, and I'm glad. You *have* to get out of your comfort zone. You *have* to push yourself. After all, you will get better *only* when you help yourself.

Sure, there will be days when you may feel hopeless. But know that it's just a fleeting feeling. You have to snap out of it for your mental well-being.

Look forward to all the good things that are waiting for you.

Practice makes perfect. Keep repeating the physical motions until they become a second habit—a muscle memory. The harder you try, the luckier you'll get. You will be pleasantly surprised by your potential. Soon, "I can't do it" will be replaced by "I can." This mental shift in your thinking will reap enormous rewards.

Modify the famous Kennedy quote—"ask not what your country can do, but ask what you can do for your country" to ask not what *others* can do, but ask what you can do for yourself. There are plenty of helpful souls to help you, but *you* have to take the first step.

Find a passion—something that you love to do. Something you have wanted to do since childhood but have not been able to do because daily life got in the way. I was fortunate to pursue my passion as a career before I got my stroke. As the saying goes, *you won't work a single day of your life if you love what you do.*

Set yourself a goal. You'll be surprised about the potential you have. I know I did. My passion is working on computers, developing websites, etc. I am discovering new technologies and reading about them. The internet is my new best friend. However, as I mentioned before, it was a learning process. Patience and perseverance have paid off. By no means do I claim to be an expert web developer. However, I do a decent job. After all, I'm not in the rat race of job hunting. I'm not striving to compete with other qualified candidates. I'm perfectly satisfied with what I've achieved. Just like what I've done, find your own comfort zone. The biggest asset one can have is to know one's limitations.

I wear two hats. Sometimes, I'm a user—a consumer—who surfs the web for information. I hem and haw, bitch and moan, shake my head, curse under my breath when something on a website doesn't work, just like a typical user would. At other times, I'm a web developer searching for a solution, thinking about how I would have tackled this differently.

However, under both circumstances, I've found that I lose myself when immersed in them. Time flies. It has, and my wife complains many times, become an addiction. I need my fix. Fortunately, it's not a bad habit to have. I spend hours at my desk, lost in the labyrinth of the World Wide Web. Thankfully, the watch on my wrist senses that my body has been inactive for a while and reminds me that I need to get up and walk.

My other passion is reading; I devour books, blog articles, magazine articles, newspaper articles, etc. However, in this era of digital devices, I prefer online materials over print media.

Like millions of Indians, I am a crazy cricket fan. Before my stroke, I was a good player, but I still enjoy watching it on TV.

I am aware that I might have repeated myself several times. I probably have said the same thing many times to drive home a point. However, in my defense, this is not fiction. This is my life story.

How do I think? How do I make sense of my situation?

Well ... as a passionate cricket lover who always bleeds blue (Indian cricket fans would get it), let me put it in cricketing terms: *I'm not out...just retired hurt.*

What motivated me to write this book?

By now, you might be wondering the reason to bare my soul. It's a perfectly valid question. If I were merely a reader reading this book, I, too, would have wondered the same. After all, don't we all have a secret compartment safely tucked away in our brains? So, it's a very valid question. Writing this book has been a mentally rewarding journey for me. It has been a walk down memory lane. There were many instances I had forgotten…well…not forgotten but had shoved it somewhere in the maze of my memory. Writing this book helped me bring it to the front. Pouring my thoughts out surprised even me about what my body had been through. It indeed has been therapeutic.

Also, although many of my close friends and family members knew my story, they were probably unaware of my entire saga … especially in India. And, of course, strangers don't know anything.

As you probably have guessed from my writing style, I'm neither a writer nor claim to be one. I just want to narrate my experiences and hope that they help someone. Even if I can make a difference in a single person's life, I'd consider that a success. When I started to write it, as I poured my thoughts down, I didn't want to turn off an average reader by using bombastic language (not that I know how to use it, but you get my point). After all, I graduated in Physics, not in English Literature. Besides, being a programmer, I tend to use minimalistic words or shortcuts to get my point across. Having gone through the horrible experience of being unable to express my thoughts in spoken words, I know how important it is to communicate. It really doesn't matter to me if one is a good orator. It's more important to convey what one is trying to say.

To me, writing is more like a science than art. I was more curious about the tools I had at my disposal that I could use. If you feel like sharing your experience—or any other thoughts (even if they are criticisms), I'd love to hear from you. Please do not hesitate to write to me at **author@thegalaxyseries.com**. I'm easily accessible via email.

I'm not a famous author or a celebrity—with millions of followers on social media, who can be challenging to reach. I feel many celebrities on social media have added pressure—in addition to looking good—to post regularly to their millions of followers.

It indeed has been a long and difficult—to say the least—journey, but it's worth it. A positive frame of mind has helped me a lot. During the day, I have occupied my mind in many activities, so I look forward to a restful sleep at the end of each day. Every morning, I have a mental checklist of what I want to achieve during the day, and at the end of the day, I mentally check off items. Sure, there are many days I've not been able to check them all. However, each check has been more gratifying than the previous one. If you've not already done so, I recommend you try it.

The other thing I had to overcome was writing a book in English, which is not my first language. I'm sure many readers will poke a hole in my grammar, sentence construction, etc. But I'm not bothered by it. The most important thing to me was to communicate—to communicate my point in a simple and easy-to-understand language. I hope I've achieved that.

Personally, not only I am proud of the way I handled my situation, but I am also prouder of being able to narrate my story in English, as it is a second language (ESL). Well, I'd consider it a third language as my mother tongue is Gujarati, and so was my primary education until the tenth grade. The national language in India is Hindi. Also, I am from Mumbai, a city in the state of Maharashtra. The state language there is Marathi (each state in India has its own language in its unique script). Although, I must confess that I'm not fluent in it.

As you may be aware, India is one of the most linguistically diverse countries in the world, with a wide range of languages and dialects spoken. The number of languages spoken in India is disputed, with some sources claiming there are 780 languages while others say there are over 19,500. Only twenty-two languages are officially recognized by its constitution.

> Dear reader, you see, many times, I may be thinking in a non-English language while translating my thoughts into English. However, there are many nations worldwide where English is not a primary language.
>
> When I was working on my very first book, India Was One, I emailed the first draft to my brother in

India. I remember one of his comments: "You tend to think in Hindi and write in English." Of course, he was right, but in my defense, multiple languages swirl in my brain. Many times, the literal translation loses its meaning—a *Lost-in-Translation* symptom.

When I wanted to narrate this story, my wife asked me if I wanted to relive the traumatic experience again. Actually, to me, it's not traumatic now, as I have come out on the other end. Enough time had passed since the mishap. I felt that it was ripe to tell my story. I am unsure if I'd feel the same way if I had to write a few years earlier. Writing is an emotional journey and not a mechanical one.

I'm not bound by a contract requiring me to publish one book yearly. Many famous authors have done this, and, as a result, their writing has degraded. They are no longer my favorite authors.

Once again, I go off on a tangent. (Proof that I'm not a writer.)

Returning to my story, it has been one helluva rollercoaster ride with many stops. People have joined me, and some have disembarked—never to be seen again. However, most have stuck by me, leaving an indelible mark in my memory.

If you are a therapist, a doctor, or a nurse, be a Christy, Sheryl, Susan, Charlie, Dr. Adams, Dr. Ikeda, Dr. Arun Amar, Cee, or one of the many wonderful souls who have impacted my life. It has been so long that some may have forgotten me, but I remember them. My very first interaction with them was twenty-four years ago, and I continue to do so with some of them even now.

When I started this arduous journey, I was thirty-six. Now, I am sixty and still have a long way to go. However, who has seen tomorrow? So, instead of delving into the past and worrying about the future, I've decided to enjoy my present. You should try it, too; it's fun.

To put it into cricketing terms, I'm in the second inning of my life. I got out cheaply in the first innings. Now, I'm in the rebuilding phase to stay long at the crease.

The human body is a fantastic entity. It will surprise you. Its ability to heal is astounding. It just needs time and proper care. And the brain is even more impressive. Its ability to learn new things is simply infinite. Take me, for example. Not only have I retrained it to issue the proper commands to my body, but I have also learned new technologies. Before I fell sick, I did not know how to develop websites. Now I do. The biggest lesson I've learned is to know that I don't know everything. That has opened my mind to new ideas. As the saying goes, *the only constant is change.* Instead of being intimidated by the unknown, I've embraced it wholeheartedly. Sure, it hasn't always worked for me, but it has been magical whenever it has.

I must confess that I initially hesitated to go to an unknown environment. However, I've noticed that once I overcome the mental block of feeling uncomfortable about my condition in a new environment, things become much more accessible. Everyone's very patient and gives me space, especially in this country. I never feel rushed. The infrastructure here is very robust.

Timely emergency services, a robust health care system, plenty of therapies, and, above all, the love and care from family and friends have significantly impacted my recovery.

I hope those who have been unfortunate enough to experience a stroke can be inspired by it. You may have been dealt a bad hand. It's entirely up to you to turn it into a winning one. There are no shortcuts in life. Instead of being in a hurry to reach the destination, enjoy the journey.

There is no substitution for hard work. As I've said earlier, the harder you work, the luckier you'll get.

Time heals—if not everything, many things. As it progresses, you will look back and see how far you have come.

*_*_*

Thank you for reading my memoir. If you enjoyed the read, please leave a review on Amazon.

Acknowledgment

Unlike well-known authors with a team of professionals, such as editors, designers, proofreaders, publishers, and promoters, my experience as an indie author was different. My family and friends assisted me in proofreading the book and offered their insights.

I thank my brother Rahul, his wife Kamala, and my friends Bharat, Shiva, and Sunil for their invaluable feedback. I wrote my book using Scrivener, and Anne Rainbow from ScrivenerVirgin (www.scrivenervirgin.com) provided guidance on several technical and editing aspects. Thank you, Cathy Speight, for your invaluable input.

While the story is ultimately mine, these individuals greatly contributed to my work.

purpleturtle.app

Other Books

1. India Was One
What if your country is divided?

Website: indiawasone.com
Facebook: facebook.com/indiawasone

2. Beyond The Milky Way - Book #1 of The Galaxy Series
A science fiction that makes us question our existence.

3. Return To Earth - Book #2 of The Galaxy Series
A science fiction with a futuristic view..

4. Divided States of America - Book #3 of The Galaxy Series
A look into our future.

5. 2120 - Book #4 of The Galaxy Series
A look into our future.

6. The Man From Afghanistan
An International Adventure.

7. Confessions of An Indian Immigrant
Dawn of IT Opportunities in the Land of Promise.

Website: thegalaxyseries.com
Facebook: facebook.com/thegalaxyseriesbooks